God Willing

How to survive expat life in Qatar

Mikolai Napieralski

Published by American 80s

Text © Mikolai Napieralski 2017

Email mikolai.napieralski@gmail.com for further information

Cover design by Alisha Jensen

With thanks to the many lifelong friends I met while in Qatar.

Contents

Welcome to the Desert

I was standing by the side of the road, on the edge of the desert, scanning the horizon for signs of a cab.

It was January 2012, sometime around dawn. I had been in Qatar for a few weeks, and I was starting to understand that the country's strict Muslim façade didn't have much to do with the day-to-day reality.

The previous night had started innocently enough. I'd been invited to drinks at a hotel bar with a few new arrivals. They'd just joined a local architecture firm, and were being shown around town by their Qatari boss. A private table had been booked at a hotel bar, and I was to meet everyone around 9pm.

It was a solid, respectable plan. But like a lot of things in Qatar, it went sideways pretty quickly, and got weird soon thereafter. By midnight we had abandoned the cocktail bar for a VIP table at the upstairs nightclub. As the drinks flowed and the tequila shots came out, the Qatari boss started passing around bumps of coke and hitting on his new female staff.

Dressed in jeans and a button-up shirt, he looked just like the other middle-aged Arabs sliding around the dance floor with a bottle of champagne in one hand, and a twenty-something girl in the other. When the club lights eventually came on at 2:30am he insisted we continue the party. That meant piling into his luxury SUV and holding on for life as he drunkenly swerved through city traffic, the suburbs and vast industrial stretches before pulling up outside a rundown block of apartments on the edge of the desert.

We knocked on one of the doors, there was a brief discussion in Arabic, and we were all ushered into a cramped living room full of Sudanese guys rolling weed and watching hip hop videos while random Eastern European girls hung around looking bored.

The Qatari boss disappeared into a side room with one of his new female staff soon after, leaving me with a joint in my hand, a room full of strangers and growing sense of unease. More guys showed up soon after, and the atmosphere gradually began to shift from drunken after-party to something more menacing and paranoid.

When one of the Sudanese guys began demanding everyone's name and who had invited them, I decided it was probably time to up and leave. A fight in the kitchen provided a suitable distraction, and I used the opportunity to slip out the back door and begin walking back towards town. It would be almost an hour before a cab came past…

I spent three years in Qatar, working for a government-funded arts institution before returning home to Australia. And the one thing that always struck me was the huge disparity between daily life and my expectations going in.

Qatar's online presence and the books I'd read before heading over, all painted the country as a safe, but boring, construction site. A developing nation where middle-aged British oil workers lived in compounds, the locals kept to themselves, and the most fun thing you could do a Friday night was catch a plane somewhere else. I quickly came to realise that wasn't the case.

By 2012 Qatar was riding the crest of a huge and powerful wave. Rich beyond its wildest dreams, the country was leveraging its oil and gas reserves to drag itself into the 21st century. And just like Dubai before it, the country was moving at breakneck speed, trying to cram a century worth of social and economic progress into a short window of opportunity.

What had begun in 1995 with the arrival of a new Emir and his modernisation agenda had slowly gathered momentum, and when Qatar was named the host of the 2022 FIFA World Cup, it formally introduced this small but wealthy kingdom to the rest of the world.

But what the outside world couldn't see, and what the new hotels, shopping malls and construction efforts helped obscure, was the social upheaval taking in Qatar.

Bedouin tribes, which had etched out a sparse desert existence for centuries, suddenly found themselves trying to navigate a path between their religious roots and the allure of the modern world.

This book attempts to capture that brief moment in time. The uneasy mix of money, ambition and religion that all came together when a wealthy, but isolated kingdom, opened its doors to the world.

Qatar's moment in the sun may have dimmed, but as work continues on the 2022 FIFA World Cup, and a new generation of westerners is brought across to manage affairs, I hope this book provides some insight and guidance to those who find themselves touching down in the desert in the years to come.

From the hotel bars and drunken brunches, to the boardrooms and crumbling neighbourhood bodegas, this is the real Qatar.

Section 1. All About Qatar

---Qatar Explained---

A Brief History of Qatar

While the Qatari peninsula has been home to nomadic tribes for thousands of years, the country's 'proper' history begins in the early 18ᵗʰ century, when a Kuwaiti tribe migrated and established the coastal town of Zubarah. Located in the country's northwest, it quickly became a bustling port and the centre of the Gulf's pearling industry.

These chill vibes were shattered in 1783 when the Al Khalifa family from neighbouring Bahrain invaded and annexed the Qatar Peninsula. A local resistance movement sprung up to ward off the invading forces, and in 1825 the House of Thani, established under Sheikh Mohammed bin Thani, became the focal point for Qatari independence.

Bahrain sent a fleet across the narrow strait in 1867 to suppress this uprising, and although their forces made it as far as Doha (the current capital), the British ultimately stepped in and negotiated a peace treaty that recognised Sheikh Mohammed bin Thani as the rightful representative of Qatar. The country formally announced its independence in 1878.

While this ended hostilities with Bahrain, Qatar still had to face incursions from the expanding Ottoman Empire. This all came to a head in an 1893 battle which saw Qatari forces beat back Turkish troops and, in the process, gain autonomy over the peninsula.

Ottoman dominance would continue to decline in the region over the next two decades, eventually collapsing during the First World War. This regional power vacuum saw Qatar become a British protectorate in 1916 — a designation it would maintain until 1971.

The 20th Century 'til today

Qatar may have gained independence at the start of the 20th century, but no one gave the place a second thought. An impoverished, sparsely populated outpost in the Gulf, the country relied on pearling for its exports and when the Japanese invented pearl farms in the 1930s, the country's slide into irrelevance took another step forward.

Things looked pretty bleak at this point — a tiny population, a barren desert climate and no source of income beyond sustenance fishing. All that changed with the discovery of vast, untapped oil reserves in the 1940s. The subsequent development of the oil industry following the Second World War saw Qatar become massively wealthy, and paved the way for the country's gradual modernisation.

All this played out against Britain's collapsing colonial empire. By the late 1960s the British had accepted that they couldn't afford to maintain their foreign outposts, and granted autonomy to many of these countries. Qatar was originally in discussions with Bahrain and what would become the United Arab Emirates to form one unified country, but when these talks stalled they decided to go it alone and on the 3rd September 1971, Qatar became a fully independent state.

Still, the country's 'great leap forward' didn't occur until 1995, when the Emir was displaced in a bloodless coup by this son, Sheikh Hamad bin Khalifa Al Thani. The new leader recognised that the country's long-term future (and security) depended on more than just oil and natural gas. In response, he initiated a series of nation-building projects that aimed to position Qatar as a sort of Middle Eastern Switzerland — a neutral powerbroker for regional conflicts.

Under his leadership, the country saw its population skyrocket from 700,000 people in 2004 to more than 2 million in 2013. This was accompanied by a new emphasis on 'soft power', with the establishment of Al Jazeera, the Doha Film Institute and Qatar Museums helping to sell the country to an international audience.

In a move largely unprecedented in the region, the Emir stepped down in 2013, and handed power to his son, Sheik Tamim bin Hamad Al Thani.

What Exactly is a Bedouin?

Qatar's indigenous population belongs to an ethnic group known as Bedouins. This is derived from the Arabic word *Badawiyin* and simply means desert dweller.

While westerners tend to view all Arabs as a singular 'race', this is, of course, ridiculous. It's like suggesting all of Europe shares the same cultural traits and world-view.

Still, the Bedouins are unique, even among Arab people. While other groups settled and built cities, the Bedouins retained their nomadic lifestyle — traveling in camel convoys and living in desert tents — well into the 20th century.

These tribal roots form the basis of Bedouin culture, and continue to pervade contemporary society. In the process they form their own unofficial class system, which is stratified according to tribal affiliation, religious sect and lineage.

In simple terms, your family name helps other Qataris identify where you sit on the country's very regimented social scale.

This tribal mentality has survived hundreds of years and is still (for better or worse), a crucial aspect of Qatari life. It lives on in a local quote: "I against my brother, my brothers and I against my cousins, then my cousins and I against strangers."

Or, to put it another way, blood is thicker than water.

In a culture where no one wants to 'rock the boat', people continue to rely on this tribal system for everything from jobs to marriage. And speaking of marriage, it's customary for matches to be found within the same bloodline — so cousins marrying cousins is still very much a thing out here. Until recently most married couples continued to live in the same multi-generational compound.

Of course all the above simply reinforces long held traditions, draws tribal groups closer together and closes off Qatari society to the wider world.

Even though the last Bedouin tribes gave up their nomadic lifestyles for fixed addresses back in the 1950s, those traditions run deep, and so do the tight knit, extended family groups at the centre of everyday life.

Being invited into a Qatari's home is therefore a big deal. You can live here for several years and barely move beyond cordial hellos with fellow Qatari employees. And it's not like they're trying to be rude, they're just wary of expats that come and go like the seasons and have very different lifestyles.

Abayas and the Thobe

From a Fox News perspective, it's easy to view the Qatari national outfits as religious garments. The truth is there's more to it than that.

It is generally accepted that the Hijab (the headscarf that covers a women's hair) is a symbol of religious adherence to Islam, while the abaya (black cloth that covers the body) is a cultural artefact rather than a religious one.

This makes a lot more sense when you consider the Bedouin's nomadic, desert dwelling heritage. If you're going to spend all that time trekking through harsh desert plains, a covering garment makes much more sense than a Sunday dress.

Whether the abaya and hijab are empowering, a personal choice or an oppressive tool that "alienates women under the guise of religious freedom" is an argument for another time and place. But making generalisations about individuals in Qatar based on their outfit is as short-sighted and lazy as doing it about the residents of New Jersey or Berlin... Although when you see a woman in an abaya and stripper heels you can't help but wonder.

Moving on...

Qatari men generally wear a thobe in public. You'll know it as that ankle-length white garment that resembles a nightgown or tunic. It's usually complemented by the ghutra (a loose headdress, usually white or red and checkered). This is held in place with a black rope known as the agal.

Now to the causal western observer a thobe is a thobe is a thobe; but there's actually a world of difference between them. From fabric, to cut, to button arrangement and general fit, a thobe is as distinct (or similar) as a business suit. The same goes for the ghutra and the way it's positioned on someone's head.

If you know what you're looking for you can guess a person's country of origin, their tribal prominence, wealth and prestige by giving their outfit a quick once over. Again, this isn't too dissimilar to the west, where a suit and tie combo can also provide plenty of hints about a person's social standing.

Oh, and a random bit of trivia, that black rope that holds the ghutra in place was at one time used to secure a camel's feet together at night, so they wouldn't wonder off.

While there's no rule saying you can't wear a thobe as a western expat, it's probably best to avoid that scenario. First up, it's assumed that anyone in a thobe speaks Arabic, so if your local language knowledge doesn't extend beyond "InShaAllah", you'll look like an asshole.

There's also the uncomfortable spectre of 'cultural tourism'. Suddenly switching from a suit and tie to a thobe can come across as a little insensitive.

Basically, it's very hard to pull off a thobe as a white western expat with limited Arabic skills and not look like you're rehearsing a Halloween outfit. If you want to show your solidarity with the locals you're better off buying a LandCruiser and taking some language lessons.

Qatar's Heart of Darkness

For a small country with a short history, Qatar punches well above its weight division. Between the upcoming FIFA World Cup, the success of Al Jazeera News, and the piles of money being thrown at international art and real estate markets, the country has turned its oil and gas reserves into global recognition.

That's all fine and good, but the country's international standing is less than 'peachy'. Generally speaking, Qatar is viewed as the backward cousin who stumbled into money, moved to the big city, and is now desperately trying to justify his presence as more than dumb luck. Or the plotline to *The Beverly Hillbillies...*

Obviously, this is not an assessment that sits well with the locals.

In their mind, the oil and the associated wealth is both a manifestation of God's favour, and a tool to be welded in his name. Whether that means buying Ferraris, funding covert wars in neighbouring countries or enslaving Filipino maids is largely irrelevant. God provided the oil and money, spending it is part of his plan, and any attempts at criticising Qatar for doing so is like criticising God himself.

This is all very neat and convenient when it's contained within a local bubble and reinforced by state media, but it quickly falls apart under international scrutiny. Which is precisely what happened when Qatar was awarded the 2022 FIFA World Cup. Overnight the kingdom went from relative obscurity to intense media focus and, much to the local's surprise, the appraisal was far from glowing.

Articles about modern-day slave labour, media censorship and the limited rights of women highlighted the dark side of Qatar's social fabric, and told uncomfortable stories. For a country that was only used to hearing how wonderful it was, the international criticism caused confusion and howling outrage. Because how could Qatar be wrong if it was doing God's will?

This leads us down an existential rabbit hole and into Qatar's very own heart of darkness; what if all the oil and money isn't a personal high-five from God, but a random accident of history?

Since nobody wants to entertain that terrifying reality, the country overcompensates, treating any accomplishment (no matter how modest), as though it was divine confirmation of Qatar's worthiness.

This creates a cheer squad mentality and means boring concepts like talent, experience and humility are swept aside in the rush to celebrate and promote anything Qataris do.

It's why government employees feel a 9am to 2pm work day is reasonable, why college graduates feel they should be parachuted into managerial roles and why any criticisms from the foreign press regarding these practises is treated as a personal insult.

Or to put it another way, "If God didn't want us to [insert dubious activity], he wouldn't have given us the oil to do it."

---Politics in Qatar---

Let's Talk About It

Or better yet, let's not... While politics can be a touchy subject at the best of times, the Middle East manages to up the crazy by several orders of magnitude. And that's just amongst locals with different opinions. As an infidel outsider your opinion means absolutely zero. It's not going to change anyone's mind about ANYTHING.

Firstly, it's extremely bad form to criticise the royal family — doing so is the quickest way to get yourself bundled onto a plane and deported. If anyone asks, the Emir is a super chill bro. End of story.

Islam is also super chill. It's an inescapable part of daily life in Qatar and, as you may have noticed, kind of a 'big deal' in the Middle East. Any criticism of the religion, the prophet Mohammed, or similar, is a sure fire way to get yourself fired / locked up / deported. If you need to have this explained to you then you probably shouldn't be in the Gulf.

Foreign military intervention is another touchy subject. Whatever your personal thoughts on the matter (and whatever you picked up via western news outlets), the region has a long and complicated history of western occupation (dating back to the crusades). The nuances of all this, and how it affects modern geopolitics is beyond this book. Or any book...

Basically, chest-thumping nationalism (or condescending talk of 'foreign aid' and intervention) will not go over well with a local audience. If you are asked to offer an opinion, and can't make a hasty exit, then at least try and phrase it within the context of your western media influence.

This seems to be especially problematic for U.S. expats. While other countries are happy to simply plunder wealth (Britain) or sleep with the locals (Spain and Portugal), there's a certain U.S. contingent that feels the need to 'fix the world's problems'.

This will manifest itself in tedious dinner party conversations about worker's rights, women's rights, gay rights, etc., etc. Yes, these are all valid concerns, but they're unlikely to be solved via a combination of watered-down beers, liberal arts idealism and 'American Exceptionalism'.

Now obviously you can't lump all foreign nationals under the same umbrella. But be wary of anyone who starts talking about 'making a difference'. They will, inevitably, be the first to become disillusioned, 'catch feelings' and leave the country.

Other Topics to Avoid

Sunni and Shia Muslims
Just, don't. Do not get into this conversation. Do not offer your opinion on this topic. If you get cornered simply nod in agreement with whatever the person says and excuse yourself as quickly as possible. Seriously, you don't want to get into a conversation about the 1500-year blood feud regarding Mohammed's rightful heir.

The U.S. military presence
While Qataris are more tolerant of western military intervention than other Middle East countries, this has a lot to do with the giant (not very secret) U.S. airbase in the middle of the country. This is to keep Saudi or Iran from getting any 'ideas'. Before the U.S. showed up, the country was under the 'protection' of the British Empire. In any case, it's a touchy subject and doesn't make for polite dinner conversation.

Western Imperialism and Middle East intervention
While the Qataris can (grudgingly) see the benefit of having the U.S. army on their soil to keep neighbouring countries at bay, broader intervention in the region makes everyone deeply suspicious. People assume that western powers are in the region to steal the oil and tell everyone what to do. Which, perhaps, isn't that far removed from the truth.

Israel
Yeah, nah. Unless your view is sympathetic to the Palestinian cause, keep your mouth shut about Israel. And even then, it's probably best to change the subject. International maps distributed in Qatar don't even include Israel – that should tell you how well regarded the country is. If the Palestine / Israel issue is complicated in the west, it's a circle jerk in Qatar (and the broader) Middle East.

Qatar's Relationship with its Neighbours

Iran
The relationship between Qatar and Iran can be summarised by the Persian Gulf / Arabic Gulf naming controversy. While only 50 kilometres of water separate the two countries, the Arabs and the Persians consider themselves entirely different people and have been in various shades of conflict for centuries.

When a Qatari government institution uploaded a map referencing the 'Persian Gulf' to its official website all hell broke lose. The CEO himself became involved, and the offending map was promptly removed — because obviously it's the 'Arab Gulf'.

Really, all you need to know is that they don't like each other.

Dubai and the U.A.E.
The U.A.E. is infinitely better than Qatar. Anyone who disagrees has not spent any time in the U.A.E., or is just being contrary. At the very least, the U.A.E. feels like a 'finished' version of Qatar — a place where the roads are not a giant construction site, the taxi drivers aren't looking to screw you over, and the government is less likely to change laws on a whim. Try telling that to a Qatari and they won't be impressed.

While it's acceptable to talk about Dubai's superior shopping, this is about as far as you can go before sliding down a very slippery slope. If you do find yourself in trouble, you can always back peddle with something like, "Qatar is still developing and can learn from Dubai's mistakes."

Saudi
The relationship between Saudi and Qatar is a long and strained one. The basic assumption is that Saudi would happily swallow up Qatar and its oil reserves if it had the chance (and relegate all its women back to the kitchen in the process).

Bahrain
Bahrain is basically a staging ground for the proxy war between Iran and Saudi. It's also home to a U.S. naval base, and before Dubai became 'a thing' it was the Middle East's preferred 'whore house' — the sort of place where 'quiet' Saturday nights conclude in faux Irish pubs surrounded by hookers.

In other words, it's the runt of the litter; the smallest and weakest country in the region, and the Gulf's whipping boy. But if you're looking for nice cocktail bars, neighbourhood restaurants serving wine, drive-through bottle shops and reasonably priced whores, it's great.

Really though, more people should visit Bahrain. And the Qataris are pretty chill about the place, since their great, great grandparents largely migrated from there on boats back in the 19th century

Note: the following is liable to change at any point for no apparent reason.

Slavery in the Gulf – Then and Now

Slavery was only outlawed in Qatar in 1952. In neighbouring gulf countries it was allowed up until the 1960s. If that seems rather late in the piece it's because it is. Most other countries outlawed slavery more than 100 years prior.

Explaining the Middle East's ongoing fondness for slavery is well beyond the scope of this book. But a little background can help place Qatar's attitude towards migrant workers in some context.

1. Slavery has been in use throughout the Arab world since pre Islamic times.

2. The Qu'ran is pretty much fine with it.

In other words, slavery was the social norm until very recently. The most obvious manifestation of this can be found in the country's labour laws, and the Kafala system that ties all foreign workers to a local sponsor.

As discussed in more detail later in the book, all foreign workers enter the country under a sponsor's name. That same sponsor can control a person's right to leave the country, find another job and various other things we take for granted in the west.

What few people realise is that the same exact rules apply to white-collar professionals from the U.S. or the U.K. as their third-world counterparts. The difference being that western workers are far less susceptible to exploitation, and are generally well compensated for their loss of liberties.

None of this is particularly strange from a traditional Middle Eastern perspective. Rewind a couple of hundred years and today's western expats would be considered 'foreign guests' of the royal courts. The migrant labourers would be slaves.

While the plight of third-world labourers causes much handwringing and pearl clutching in the west, it's mostly a none-issue in the Gulf. Due to the deeply ingrained tradition of slavery, many Qataris see no problem with the country's treatment of these poor bastards. After all, "they chose to come here and they're getting paid money to work."

Meanwhile, inconvenient truths like the confiscation of passports, withheld wages and 'agent fees' which see people arrive heavily in debt are dismissed as details or isolated incidents.

Western expats find this attitude mystifying. After all, Qatar is one of the world's wealthiest nations and can afford to pay labourers a fair wage. It's a topic of conversation that will come up repeatedly and be met with a familiar mix of outrage, indignation and a grudging acceptance of 'cultural differences'.

If it's something that the locals worry about they keep it to themselves. The general consensus is that any push to change the system is intended to placate foreign interest, rather than legitimate internal concern.

---Qataris and Expats---

Qatar's Class System

If you come from a western country you're probably used to the vague notion that everyone is essentially 'equal'. Sure, some people earn more money or come from more privileged backgrounds, but there's the underlying assumption that people from different nationalities and socioeconomic backgrounds can come together and have a drink when the situation requires it.

That sort of freedom simply doesn't exist in Qatar. The country has an extremely rigid class system that ensures people stick within their own groups. So no matter how liberal or open minded you might be, you'll quickly discover that all your friends come from suspiciously similar backgrounds. It's not your fault.

Here's the thing, Qatar has a population of approximately 2 million people. But only about 300,000 are Qatari. The rest are foreign workers brought in to help create all the shopping malls, football stadiums and infrastructure you start demanding when you fall ass backwards into oil money.

That's great and all, but it means the Qataris are a minority in their own country. And that makes them very nervous. Because what was once a quiet backwater is now home to a bunch of Pakistani, Indian, Nepalese and African labourers building gleaming monuments to consumerism that they'll neve be able to afford. Which, if you've read much history, is a scenario that tends to end badly for the ruling class.

But we're getting off topic…

This influx of foreigners has given Qatar (and the rest of the Gulf) a five-tier society that breaks down like this:

1. Qataris

At the very top you'll find the Qataris. To compensate for all the construction work and foreigner workers loitering about, they're lavished with interest-free loans, government subsidised housing and public sector jobs that require little more than showing up.

2. Western Expats

Below the locals you'll find professional western expats who are enticed to Qatar with large (tax-free) salaries and the promise of adventure. If you're reading this book you'll most likely fall into this category.

3. North African Expats

A lot of the Gulf's administrative work is handled by a professional class of North African expats. Because they're Muslim, and from the neighbouring region, they tend to tick a lot of the right boxes. Plus, they work for cheap, since their own economies are perpetually in the toilet. But they're also African, which means they're considered racially inferior to the Arabs and forever stuck in Middle Management.

4. Asian Retail Staff

The country's retail and service staff are almost exclusively from the Philippines. They're here to earn a buck and send it back to their family. They have their own neighbourhoods and shops, and deal with all the bullshit they encounter out here with a lot of karaoke.

5. South Asian Labourers and Workers

At the bottom of this social rung you'll find the labourers and migrant workers. They're here to do all the jobs that are too boring, dangerous or just plain ridiculous for anyone else to bother with. When you heard stories about indentured labour and modern-day slavery in the Gulf it's referring to these poor saps.

The Asian Tea Ladies

Visit any office building in Qatar and you'll find small kitchenettes staffed by Filipino women whose sole job is to make teas and coffees for the white-collar workers.

The women sit in these tiny, cramped rooms from 7:30am to 2:30pm listening to Jesus hymns on tiny transistor radios and getting in your way when you try and get something out of the fridge.

If you work in a government building there's usually one kitchenette per floor, with at least two women assigned to run it. There's also a 'main dude', who's the boss of these tea ladies. His job is to appear twice a day with Arabic coffee. He brings this around on a nice little tray with small ornate cups. Arabic coffee is an 'acquired taste'; it's sweater, served with milk and has an almost nutty flavour.

So far so weird, but the real kicker is the local attitude towards these women. As a Qatari co-worker once explained, the tea ladies "live in the closet" and "belong to the CEO."

That sort of attitude is pretty common throughout the region when it comes to the hired help. The reasoning goes something like this: these people made a conscious decision to come to this country, they perform menial tasks, they're paid crap, but they're obviously better off here than back home, so they should be happy they have this job.

Make of that what you will.

Cruising for Day Labour

When you first arrive in Qatar your main point of contact with third-world migrants will be via the backseat of a town car while they ferry you between work, cocktail lounges and your hotel.

While your natural inclination may be to develop some good-natured rapport and ask them about the city, this doesn't really work since their English is pretty basic.

The drivers can take you where you want to go and turn the air conditioner on and off. They can also tune into the local English language radio station (the audio horror show that is 97.5), but that's about it. Trying to engage them in conversation is an exercise in futility and awkwardness. Give it a week and you'll simply plug your headphones in and listen to whatever playlist you have on your phone.

While being driven around in the back of your company town car you'll encounter roundabouts where groups of men who look like Afghan peasants congregate. They're the local day labourers, and for the most part they really are from Afghanistan or Pakistan.

Qataris who need guys to build a wall, dig a hole, or construct a hotel will show up in their gigantic pick-up trucks, throw these guys in the back and pay them chump change to do whatever needs doing. At the end of the day they're dropped back off.

The whole thing is not dissimilar to the cheap migrant workers that you'll find in U.S. states neighbouring the Mexican border. Honestly, the less you know about them and their circumstances the better.

The Relationship between Qataris and Expats

The relationship between Qataris and western expats is a complex one. While there's an understanding that Qatar needs outside help to train its citizens and maximise the country's output, there's an undercurrent of resentment on both sides.

Qataris tend to view the westerners as barely qualified losers that couldn't find work back home. Americans and Brits are considered pushy and amoral with no respect for local customs. Oh, and they're only out here for the money.

Meanwhile, the westerners think of Qataris as spoilt and lazy, and assume the whole country would grind to a halt if they weren't here to prop it up.

Both are gross generalisations, but they'll give you an insight into the misunderstandings that govern these relationships.

The one thing everyone can agree on is that Qatari needs a foreign workforce to build and manage its geo-political ambitions. And when it comes to soft power, the country's push to create a regional arts and museums hub has only been surpassed by the FIFA world cup in 2022 and the expansion of Al Jazeera.

All three ventures have received plenty of international attention and their fair share of drama. They've also been plagued by the aforementioned cultural tensions.

When Worlds Collide

A government department Story (abridged)

Qatar Museums has spent the past decade developing the country's burgeoning arts scene. That's meant importing a bunch of western professionals to manage the museums, train the locals and provided specialist services.

In theory, this makes sense. It helps fast track the development of cultural institutions and the local professionals to run them. Unfortunately, the reality has been plagued by tears, lawsuits, staff dismissals and abandoned projects.

At least some of the blame can be attributed to Qatar's class system and the sort of workplace environments it produces. These issues are not unique to the arts sector, and the following points apply to any government-affiliated workplace.

1. Wages aren't equal. Qataris get paid far more for the same position than their expat colleagues. So what you

end up with is junior Qatari staff earning more than their supervisors.

2. A very different work ethic. Qatari staff are much more relaxed about deadlines and their implications. This can be traced back to the local tradition of *InShaAllah* – i.e. 'God Willing'. The phrase is thrown around with reckless abandon, and it drives western management to despair because its literal translation is, 'If I feel like it'.

3. Two sets of office hours. Speaking of deadlines, most Qatari employees in government jobs will leave at 2pm sharp [the official closing time] regardless of whether an urgent job has been finished or not. That leaves the expat staff to stay back and ensure things get done. Qatari staff are also entitled to take casual days for 'religious fasting'.

4. Staff employed for the hell of it. Qatar has virtually zero unemployment. The country achieves this by pushing the slacker locals into fictional jobs that barely exist. In Qatar Museums the HR department was largely comprised of employees who didn't want to work and would sit around watching YouTube videos and lunching between 8am and 2pm. What you end up with is a department of 30 people in which maybe 10 do the actual work.

5. It's impossible to fire someone. There was a local woman at a certain government department who simply didn't show up to work. She was foisted in there for some imaginary job, didn't report to anyone, didn't have any tasks to do and would show up maybe one or two days a month. There was absolutely nothing the foreign manager could do aside from shifting her to a different department.

All these factors add up to create highly dysfunctional organisations with huge staff, massive overheads and minimal productivity. The western expats come to resent the Qataris for their lack of productivity while the Qataris resent being told what to do by people they think are there to assist them.

Upsetting the Wrong Locals

One thing you should never forget in Qatar is that all foreigners are 'guests' of the royal family and the local population.

The western management at Qatar Museums (QM) discovered this the hard way when their attempts to streamline the organisation and 'downsize' the deadweight crashed and burned in a blaze of leaked media stories and local 'outrage'. Long story short; – the senior western managers were sent home, the deadweight locals all kept their jobs.

The following email was dispatched by a Qatar Museums staffer to friends back home in the west and proved prescient.

Bad times at QM: a letter home from a western staffer – August 2013.

An article appeared in one of the local Arabic newspapers yesterday that basically ripped the [expat] management at Qatar Museums apart. Among the claims was financial misappropriation, cover-ups, wild parties, and the fact a same-sex couple had been granted a housing allowance [the horror!].

What makes this interesting is that you can't publish hatchet job articles like this without the permission of the government. And there's been lots of weirdness and rumours swirling around QMA for months. I won't bore you guys with the details, but despite plans to go private, the organisation was suddenly placed under a government department with no official notice. Plus there's talk that our CEO Sheikha Mayassa is leaving for New York, and all the British Management [former Christie's people] are getting kicked out.

This sort of open attack in the media is normally what happens before the government moves in, sacks all the management, gets their own goons in and charges senior management with vague crimes. None of which is maybe that exciting for you guys on the other side of the world, but it does provide a glimpse into how things work out here. Like, some communist-era purges...

The funny thing is the original article was a complete hatchet job. One example, and I'm paraphrasing, "A yoga teacher was named the head of cultural affairs".
Now while it's true the guy is a yoga teacher, that's his hobby, he's a qualified professional in his field — even if he is an asshole that everyone hates.

So while a lot of the claims might have some truth to them, they've been presented in an extremely skewed kinda way.

But yeah, I'm sure there are some very nervous management at QMA. If the government goes after you on 'financial irregularities' and charges you, you can be stuck in the country for years fighting court cases.

---Local Etiquette---

Got Wasta?

You'll hear the term *wasta* thrown around a lot in the Middle East. In polite circles it simply means 'influence' and is dismissed as harmless tradition. In a western courtroom it would be described as 'nepotism', 'corruption' and 'cronyism'. Basically, using one's connections and family name to gain some sort of competitive advantage.

It manifests itself in a variety of ways, but it's especially popular when it comes to securing lucrative government contracts, landing a job or promotion, or skipping out on traffic fines. In other words, all the stuff that would get you locked up for years if you tried it back home.

Although wasta has become little more that state-sanctioned corruption, its origins are more innocent and pragmatic. It was originally a means of settling tribal disputes and maintaining order — those with wasta were able to negotiate 'conflict resolution' before it spilled into violence. Fair enough.

More recently, it's been described as "affirmative action for the advantaged" and a way of ensuring those in power stay there at the expense of less privileged individuals. So if you're wondering why the guy fresh out of Qatar University who doesn't speak English is your new general manager you can now give it a name.

While there has been a move towards increased transparency in recent years (especially when it comes to awarding business contracts), wasta is very hard to prove. It's very nature means that cases where it has been used will never be investigated because they threaten the status quo.

Western companies in Qatar have long accepted that this is the price of doing business out here. Having a Qatari 'business partner' who automatically takes 51% of your company is standard. Big contracts sometimes require an extra push, and this is when you'll see the idiot offspring of prominent families parachuted into lucrative, important-sounding positions, which don't actually require them to do anything.

In other words, it's no different from those 'no show' jobs Tony Soprano and his crew in the TV series *Sopranos* used to doll out to friends.

Dress Standards

As the summer months approach and the temperature skyrockets, the western expats start to wear less clothing. This reminds the Qataris that they're Muslims, and that having white people flashing their knees and shoulders makes them uncomfortable.

Actually, most Qataris don't really care. But there's a small, vocal minority who is newly outraged each summer, and feels obliged to launch 'education' campaigns about what is and isn't okay with God.

Inevitably, this gets played out on social media with the two sides arguing about 'respecting local culture' vs. 'you want to be an international city you gotta accept exposed shoulders'. Or something along those lines…

It's a pointless argument, since Westerners with a fondness for summer dresses and short shorts will continue to wear them, and Qataris who want to clutch metaphorical pearls while harping on about "the children" will stay outraged.

Point being; it's not an argument you want to get involved with. You'll have a much easier life in Qatar if you save the skimpy outfits and exposed knees to hotel bars and private compounds.

Public Displays of Affection

Public displays of affection are deeply frowned upon in the Gulf. As you should already be aware, men shouldn't attempt to shake a Qatari woman's hand unless she offers it first. This stems from broader cultural issues about men interacting with females they're not related or married to and yada, yada…

We don't need to get into that here. All you really need to know is this isn't Europe, and even something as simple as a husband and wife holding hands can get 'looks'.

You should also refrain from any 'kiss on the cheek' greetings while out in public. The double-kiss is the standard greeting amongst expats in hotels and at home, but try that somewhere in public —like one of the Souqs (i.e. the standing markets) — and you can get taken aside by the local 'morality police' for a lecture about public decency.

Photos of Local Women

As you may have figured out, the Gulf is a pretty conservative place. This manifests itself in all sorts of mysterious ways. And sometimes really obvious ones — like how you're not supposed to take any photos of the local women (without their express permission).

This can be a little awkward if you're trying to take photos in a public space, e.g. at the Souq. As long as you aim the camera at a legitimate landmark and don't look like a creep, you shouldn't really have any issues with public photos, but it's something to be aware of.

It also means all the press shots from the country tend to feature a bunch of dudes. Which makes people in the west ask where all the women are (and assume they're locked up at home making babies and cooking dinner). Qatari women are actually very prevalent in everyday life — they just don't appear in photos.

When it comes to public events where photographers will be present, e.g. a press conference, Qatari women will usually avoid the more obvious photo opportunities. Or they may turn their head away and cover their faces with the niqab when a camera pans in their direction.

Depending on who is present and the nature of an event, these rules can change rather arbitrarily. Ultimately, it's not that much different to the west — you wouldn't want a random stranger taking your photo without asking your permission first. Conversely, if you're standing up publicly at an open event you kind of assume someone is going to be taking photos. The fact someone is wearing an abaya doesn't change that.

Where the photo thing does get a little weird is social media. Qatari women rarely have any pictures of themselves attached to their accounts. Add someone from work to your preferred social media network (which is a whole other minefield we won't get into here), and you'll find that your online stalking is extremely unsatisfying. All you're likely to find are pictures of their pets, their meals and some random landscape shots.

Basically, if you want to see what someone looks like under their abaya you either have to go on a business trip to a western country (the abayas usually come off mid-flight) or marry them.

A Qatari Wedding

Qataris rarely let westerns into their private lives. While you might work side-by-side and share the occasional lunch, the relationship ends with the working day.

There are lots of reasons for this, but in the interest of brevity we can lump them under 'cultural differences' and move on.

The one exception to all this is a Qatari wedding. When a Qatari woman is getting married she will invite EVERYONE to the reception. That includes a token white girl. And if you're lucky enough to get an invite you should totally go because from all accounts it's quite the scene.

Receptions will usually last several hours, give all the women in attendance a chance to wear glamorous, skin tight outfits and are basically hyper-coloured fever dreams.

Just make sure you bring another random western woman with you, or you might spend the evening nodding politely while someone's elderly aunt talks at you in Arabic.

Lining Up is for Suckers

One thing you'll quickly learn in the Gulf is that people don't line up. A smooth, orderly queue, in which everyone awaits their turn simply doesn't happen. If you want service you simply make your way to the counter and yell louder than everyone else.

While Gulf nationals are unfailing polite in most cases, the stampede to the front of a queue can throw westerners off. It's especially intimidating when you find groups of abaya-clad women going straight to the front of the queue as if you were invisible. Initially, you'll assume this is just a handful of 'bad apples' ruining it for everyone else, and so you'll attempt to keep your place in line lest the whole fabric of society collapses.

After 10 to 15 minutes of this you'll be in a rage and ready to abandon civilisation for a cottage in the woods. Or you'll just start cutting in line like everyone else. Congratulations, you've just taken a small step to assimilating.

Things get extra stroppy when you find yourself surrounded by South Asians in one of the more working-class sections of town. Wonder into a busy convenience store and you'll find twenty men yelling at the guy behind the counter while shoving money in his face. If you're lucky the clerk will take pity and serve you while the yelling builds to a feverish crescendo — because obviously everyone needs their $3 mobile phone recharge card RIGHT NOW. If that doesn't happen you're just going to have to push your way to the front and act like a jerk.

Bartering

The Middle East has a long and proud tradition of bartering. If you pay the listed price on anything you're basically a sucker. Granted, you're not going to have much luck negotiating at a hotel, department store or fancy restaurant, but everywhere else is ready to wheel and deal.

Hit up the Souqs and you should be able to halve the price of anything with a bit of practice. Here are some basic tactics to get you started:

1. Laugh at the merchant's initial price
2. Point out the inferior quality of the product
3. Act like the merchant's reluctance to drop the price is a personal insult
4. Threaten to walk away
5. Tell the merchant that lowering the price will compel you to tell all your friends about his generosity and personally deliver them to him for more sales
6. Silently stare at the merchant after quoting your final paying price.

You might feel a tinge of western guilt while performing this elaborate song and dance routine (especially since you're arguing over pennies), but it's a tradition that's been going on for millennium. And besides, who are you to fuck tradition up?

Oh, the one exception to all this is the Egyptians. They're notorious throughout the region for their hard-nosed bargaining and ability to actually increase the price of a sale. Yes, this is a gross generalisation. No, I don't care.

---Foreigners You'll Meet in Qatar---

Filipinos

There's a huge Filipino community in Qatar and most of them work in the service industry. If you walk into a retail store, supermarket or café, you'll almost certainly be served by someone from the Philippines. And there's a good chance they'll be singing, because, for whatever reason, they all really, really love to sing.

They're also extremely diligent. Most Filipinos are here to earn money for families back home. That means they work multiple jobs and live in shared accommodation. They're usually picked up in company shuttle buses in the morning, driven to work, then picked up and driven to their second (or third job) later that same day.

There are entire neighbourhoods dedicated to the local Filipino community and you'll often find them hanging around Al Sadd in the evenings, which has multiple Filipino grocery stores and fried chicken places. You'll also find them on dating websites and at Filipino-designated hotel bars — which you should definitely check out, because the drinks are a lot cheaper than elsewhere and the crowd is a wonderfully flamboyant mix of gay men, prostitutes and western expats behaving disgracefully.

Generic Middle East Expats

The Middle Eastern expats can be broken down into three distinct groups: the Lebanese, the Sudanese, and the Egyptians. And while this book hopes to avoid culturally-insensitive stereotypes, that's pretty much what we're going to do here. Sorry in advance.

Let's starts with the Lebanese, because as a mix of Muslim and Christian culture on the edge of the Mediterranean they see themselves as a distinct entity. And they're mostly correct in that regard.

The Lebanese have no time for the puritanical modesty of the Arab world, and have one of the highest rates of breast augmentation surgery in the world. You can always spot a Lebanese woman because she'll be the one wearing high heels, tight clothing and extremely heavy make-up in a sea of abayas. The men will always have two packets of Marlboro cigarettes and multiple phones in their hand at any given moment. Even in their sleep.

You'll find the local Lebanese community hanging out at nightclubs, hotel bars and Mercedes dealerships. They will often work for semi-legit financial services companies and try to sell you a timeshare.

The Sudanese (and North Africans) are a lot less fun and a lot more insular. The community tends to stick together and do its own thing away from prying eyes. They tend to work in a lot of administrative roles or security gigs. They do not socialise with the western expats; they are a mystery wrapped in a riddle that you will never understand.

The Egyptians, and other Arabs from neighbouring countries, tend to make up the merchant class. They're the ones importing and exporting goods, selling used Land Cruisers, starting businesses and the like. They're also the only ones who will openly call out a Qatari about their bullshit. Which doesn't really help you much, but it's good to know.

South Asian Labourers

As far as the general public is concerned these poor bastards are invisible. Which is really just a coping mechanism for the gross inequality they represent.

After all, it's much easier to ignore the workers than think about the fact they earn around $300 USD a month, live in shared accommodation, and are actively discriminated against by all aspects of Qatari society.

In 2012 the government passed laws that forbid 'bachelors' (as they're locally known), from living in residential areas. They're also 'discouraged' from entering local shopping malls, public parks and anywhere else their wretched poverty might inconvenience the locals. After all, you don't sit down for dinner with 'the help', and you certainly don't shop at the same store.

To help alleviate the guilt and awkwardness associated with the local labour force, Qatar has constructed a series of mini cities for them to inhabit out in the desert. Places like 'Labour City' have their own shopping centre, sports fields, entertainment options and high density housing, to help keep the South Asians contained and away from the general population.

How the labour force feels about all of this is mystery, since no one has ever thought to ask them. That's okay though, because white people have been happy to jump in and project their own feelings in various 'think pieces' for *The Guardian and* suchlike.

The European Aristocrats

Hang around in Doha long enough and you'll eventually stumble across the European aristocrat crowd. While they might look like every other expat at first glance, spend a few minutes talking to them and they'll start to drop hints about their privileged upbringing.

Oh, you play Polo? You were an amateur bullfighter in Spain? Your father is an advisor to a government minister? You spent a year studying acting in New York? You're interning for the Italian ambassador?

Money is never mentioned; it doesn't have to be. The rich have their own way of identifying each other. This can be a little intimidating if you grew up in middle class suburbia (or worse); because suddenly your childhood starts to look like a Charles Dickens novel.

Since you can't beat these people on their own terms, your best bet is to go the exact opposite route, and talk up your poverty. With a little imagination you can turn a white picket fence and family camping trips into an urban wasteland of roaming gangs, guns and drugs.

Rich kids like slumming it from time to time. The fact these people are in Doha means they obviously have a weird bent for chaos and bad infrastructure. And hey, just like every boy band needs a 'troubled rebel' (shout outs to Donnie Wahlberg), every crew of rich aristocrat kids in Doha needs someone from the wrong side of the tracks.

Besides, it's a great way to meet new and interesting people with all kinds of connections. Play your cards right and you'll be rubbing shoulders with people who can afford to bankroll your 30-second elevator pitch.

All of which is terribly cynical and probably better suited to sociopaths. But, you get the idea. Besides, if it's good enough for J. Gatsby then it's good enough for you.

Section 2: Working in Qatar

---Work and Recruitment---

Kafala Good Times!

Regardless of who you work for and how you found yourself in Qatar, you'll be employed under the country's much maligned 'Kafala' system.

In other words, you'll have a local sponsor. And whether that sponsor is an individual or an organisation, they basically own your ass.

As has been pointed out by everyone from CNN to Amnesty International, an employee needs their sponsor's permission to do anything and everything from leaving the county, to opening a bank account, renting a home, changing jobs or buying alcohol.

While the Kafala system is usually associated with the third-world labourers that make up the bulk of Qatar's workforce, the unspoken reality is it also applies to white-collar western professionals. So, basically, the people reading this book…

The only real difference is sponsors are much less likely to screw over a white person with a U.S. or British passport because a), It sends a bad message, it will end up in western papers and may scare off other potential employees and b), the governments from these countries are not entirely corrupt/useless and will actually step in if a local business owner tries to enslave a bunch of nationals.

If you were a first-year university student you would probably refer to this as 'white privilege' while writing an overwrought essay about injustice. But regardless of your views on 'sponsorship' and its potential for abuse, it's the reality for most foreigner workers in Qatar.

I say 'most', because there are a couple of ways around it. If you work for a large multi-national organisation with a satellite branch in Qatar, you can work out here under your original western contract. In this instance your company will be your 'sponsor'. Alternatively, you can come out on a tourist visa and work illegally, making 'visa runs' to Dubai every few months.

We'll look at all three options in this chapter.

Incidentally, the Kafala system isn't unique to Qatar; similar systems exist in other Middle Eastern countries. Qatar has received a lot more attention because of the FIFA World Cup 2022 and the associated scrutiny. Lebanon, Bahrain, Iraq, Jordan, Kuwait, Oman, Qatar, Saudi Arabia and the U.A.E. all have some form of sponsorship in place, although it's usually aimed at low-skill migrant workers, rather than white-collar expats.

Getting Hired (by a Private Company)

The main thing about private companies is they're not crippled by the bureaucratic deadweight that typifies the government sector. You can be interviewed for a job on Sunday and asked to start on Monday. For overseas recruits it's not unusual to be on a plane within a month.

Be aware that some smaller companies may try to bypass the official 'Kafala' system altogether when they hire you. In these cases they'll offer you a tourist visa, a contract and a paid flight. Basically, you'll be working illegally and required to do a 'visa run' to Dubai every three months to keep your passport legit.

The immigration department is familiar with these sorts of arrangements and they'll usually look the other way. Long story short; no one really cares about western professionals on semi-legit work contracts. And even if they did, no one would dare question another Qatari's business affairs or hiring procedures. It's simply not the done thing.

While these sorts of contracts free employees from the burden of a 'sponsor', they also mean you have zero legal recourse if anything goes wrong. So if your boss suddenly decides they want to slash your salary, change work hours or kick you out of the company housing, you're on your own. Oh, and you won't be eligible for a residency card, which will make things like renting an apartment or buying a car a whole lot more difficult.

Basically, you're leaving yourself open to massive exploitation if you choose to work in Qatar on a tourist visa. Which is why any halfway legitimate company (public or private) will go through the official government channels.

Architectural stories

I joined a small architectural firm in Doha on a contract (that wasn't worth the paper it was written on) and a tourist visa. I had just graduated after five years studying in the U.S. and this Qatari firm offered me the chance to work on large-scale projects that I wouldn't even get to think about back home. It all started fine, but the company was mess, the boss was a nightmare, and they let half the newly arrived staff go within six months, simply handing out flight tickets home and telling us we had three days to leave the country.

John, USA, Architect.

Getting Hired (by a Government Organisation)

A position with a Qatari government department is a lot harder to come by, but it does offer several notable benefits.

Before we get into that, it's worth noting that the hiring process can take anywhere from six months to a year. This is because Qatari government departments are notoriously laid back when it comes to things like 'work' and 'deadlines'.

Qatari locals who don't want to work (and can't be fired) are often clustered together in departments like HR. This helps maintain the country's 'full employment' credentials and allows everyone to 'save face' — perhaps the defining characteristic of Bedouin society.

It also means you end up with hundreds of employees sitting around HR departments, chatting on their phones and stubbornly ignoring the applications that come across their desks.

The only effective way to navigate this maze of indifference is to have someone on the inside that can follow up with HR and find out why it has taken them a month to look at a CV for an available position. Or failing that, you'll have to harass people until they become so sick of your emails and calls they decide to process your applications just to get rid of you.

That's just the first hurdle. Even then, you will be required to provide written, signed, stamped and authenticated copies of everything you've ever done in your life. Which leads to the next section.

A Qatar-Friendly CV

To score an expat position in a Qatari government department you'll need to jump through all sorts of hoops. The typical HR manager will require signed letters from every single job you've ever held confirming your employment status and duration.

You will also need to provide a signed affidavit from the police in your home country confirming your clean criminal record. Also, your diploma, which will need to be signed and stamped by the university in question.

The other thing to keep in mind is that your remuneration for most government jobs will be based on your 'years of experience' rather than previous roles or responsibilities. Since people are arriving in Qatar from all over the world with all sorts of different job titles, work history and experience, someone decided to 'simplify' the process by ignoring individual circumstances and assigning jobs based on years worked.

Oh, and while we're talking experience, Government departments don't recognise freelance work. It's simply not a thing. You either have a day job or you don't, and juggling several freelance writing gigs (for instance) doesn't count.

The good news is you can 'tweak' your CV to make it more palatable for your typical Qatari HR manager. With a little chutzpah and some creative job titles you can turn several years of freelance work and odd jobs into a distinguished career of solid employment.

First things first, if you held a part-time job when you graduated university then that's where you should start your employment history. If you've had several short-term careers with intermittent breaks, it might be an idea to pick the most impressive sounding and stretch out your employment time a little bit.

You'll be asked to supply letters from all these employers on official letterheads confirming your title and time of employment. Depending on your industry and employment record, half these places may have closed down years ago. Not to worry, the odds that a Qatari HR manager will pick up a phone and dial overseas to check your references is approximately zero.

What you choose to do with this information is entirely up to you. Qatari has been cracking down on fraudulent diplomas from places like India, but no one is going to check exact employment dates for a western expat. As long as your support material is based on real experiences, in real places and you're not simply making things up, the HR department is not going to go all NCIS on you. Besides, they have YouTube videos to watch.

Reject that first offer

Always reject the first offer. If your application does actually go through, the HR person responsible will almost certainly have made some sort of clerical error and sent you through an offer with the wrong job title and a half-assed salary. This back and fourth over title and salary will add another couple of months to the process, but there's always more money for those who demand it.

Working in Qatar Under a Foreign Contract

The third and final way you may end up in Qatar is via a transfer from your original employer. Larger international companies with outposts in Qatar sometimes send promising junior staff to help run operations and gain experience.

While the circumstances will vary from country to country and organisation to organisation, the basic premises remains the same — you'll stay employed by your parent company and be sponsored by their local branch.

Any international company that's large enough to open a Qatar branch will have a well established, and well-formalised HR process, so all the details regarding housing, visas, payments, taxes and superannuation will almost certainly be sorted out for you.

Also, because you're still employed by the same parent company, you won't have to worry about exit permits, No-Objection Certificates or any of the other issues that you might potentially face with a local Qatari sponsor.

So to summarise: The easiest and safest way to land yourself a gig in Qatar is to be seconded by a global corporation with a local branch. Granted, it's not as prestigious as the New York, Tokyo or Hong Kong office, but it's a great way to start your international career and often considered a testing ground for ambitious corporate types.

Housing Packages

When it comes to expat remuneration packages, every organisation has its own policies and procedures. The most important thing to keep in mind when negotiating salary and benefits is the housing (and schools, if you have kids). Rent in Qatar is ridiculously expensive and comparable to what you'd be paying somewhere like London or New York.

One-bedroom apartments in West Bay or The Pearl, i.e. places where you'll want to live, start at around USD $4000 a month (about $11,000 QR). Even an older, two-bedroom apartment with stray cats outside and dodgy neighbours can run you USD $2000 a month and be considered a bargain.

Keep this in mind when reviewing your employment offer and the 'housing allowance'. A couple of thousand bucks a month might seem like a generous top-up, but most of these figures haven't been updated in a decade and won't even begin to cover the cost of living in Doha.

If you're applying for a government position you'll often be given the choice of housing or salary allowance. Always take the housing! (See below for more details.)

Jobs in the private sector tend to pay more money, but the housing situation is a lot less generous. This is why you'll often see a group of three or four professionals sharing a place. With rent prices through the roof you can either get a couple of housemates or blow 50% of your income on the luxury of solitude.

That said, there are benefits to sharing with others. If you're new to the place and get the right mix of people together it's a great way to meet friends and get yourself a posse. It also means there's a higher likelihood of house parties and drunk people hanging out at your place, which means you can find a new 'wifey' or football player without having to brave the terrible nightclubs.

Government Housing

Government housing is not something people aspire to in the west. Qatar is not the west. Rather, it's a giant welfare state with money to burn and people to house. And the government housing is pretty damn good.

A typical mid-level government employee will receive a new two-bedroom apartment to themselves with all amenities paid for as part of their job package. If you have a family or a more senior position you can expect a three-bedroom apartment or villa.

As mentioned above, rent prices in Qatar are criminal and you would struggle to afford any of these places if you worked for the private sector. So while government salaries may appear lower on paper, housing can be worth an extra $3000 to $5000 a month if you calculate the market price of similar accommodation. Also, it means you can save yourself the indignity of living in shared accommodation in your 30s.

In other words, TAKE THE GOVERNMENT HOUSING OPTION if offered. Oh, and the some goes for company housing.

Trying to Fire a Qatari (Simply Doesn't Happen)

It is virtually impossible for a Qatari to be fired. It simply has not happened. Ever. In the whole history of the universe a local has never been fired. In the most extreme cases they get transferred to a different department or are simply told to stay home and cash cheques.

Tribal roots and family connections still run deep in this region and firing someone is perceived as an affront to the whole family. Plus, their uncle got them the job, and their sister is married to the director, and yada, yada — you get the idea.

But the real fun starts when a western director or chief officer tries to come in and shift the local deadweight. This happens every few years at the larger organisations and the result is always the same. The westerner gets fired and the locals keep their jobs.

Having a white man (or woman) show up and attempt to downsize the local population is the cultural equivalent of setting fire to the national flag while eating a pork roll. It does not go over well.

When a Qatari isn't working out in a role the standard course of action is to either promote them into some imaginary token position, or to shuffle them off to a backwater department where they can watch YouTube videos all day. Naturally, this all comes down to family connections and surname.

Just watch YouTube all day and don't make a scene

While many Qataris are hard working and genuinely wish to contribute to the improvement of their country, there are, inevitably, some 'bad apples'.

In one notable instance, a Government organisation found themselves dealing with a local woman who simply wouldn't show up to work. She had been shuffled around between departments until she found her way to the marketing team at an arts organisation. After a few days spent getting her desk looking right she disappeared – and wouldn't be seen again for weeks.

Over the next year or so she averaged 3-4 days in the office per month, even as the staff numbers ballooned and actual office space became highly sought after. The new Chief Marketing Officer was finally forced to act and called this woman in for a meeting (backed up by the head of HR and print-outs detailing computer login details and swipe card usage to confirm the chronic absenteeism).

Faced with these overwhelming and irrefutable facts, the Qatari woman simply stated that they were wrong and she was at work every day. A call was placed to the chief officer the following day from the Qatari woman's husband saying she was pregnant and was taking her government allowed (and fully paid) maternity leave effective immediately. We never did find out what happened to her...

You've Been Terminated

When it comes to western expats, the job security thing is pretty straightforward. A private company can let you go at any time for any reason. Like the actual hiring process, it's fast and almost entirely lawless.

Government positions are a different matter. The lumbering bureaucracy that sees official documents ignored, lost or misfiled works both ways. If you want to get rid of someone you're going to need a whole lot of patience and a whole lot of photocopies, because those forms you lodged were probably shredded on principle.

Generally speaking, managers will try and shuffle someone off to another department before they have to go through the slow and difficult process of reclaiming an employee's apartment, making them repay their loans and putting them on a plane.

There is one caveat to all the above — cultural insensitivity. Any hint that you have insulted the religion, the royal family or a local Qatari, and you can find yourself bundled onto a plane and sent home with remarkable speed and efficiency. Sometimes even a short stay in local prison.

No-Objection Certificate
(and Trying to Leave Your Job)

Whether you leave your organisation on good terms or are escorted out the door by security, you're going to need a No-Objection Certificate (NOC) from your sponsor if you want to continue working in Qatar.

This is part of the country's much criticised Kafala system, and means your employer (and sponsor) can basically hold your career to ransom.

Reasons why they might refuse an NOC can vary. Some of the more popular include:

- You're massively incompetent
- They don't like you or hold some weird grudge
- They feel that they have invested time and money in you and don't want to see you take those skills to a better / high paying job
- They're mentally unstable
- Just because.

Each organisation deals with NOCs differently, and there really aren't any hard or fast rules. As a western professional, you'll be 'expected' to stay with an organisation for at least two years before they're happy to let you leave, but that varies hugely depending on personal circumstances.

If they do refuse an NOC there's very little you can do about it without getting caught up in a notoriously slow and biased justice system.

Promotions and Raises

Jobs in the private sector aren't governed by any sort of (enforced) legislation, so companies are pretty much left alone to sort out their house rules. If your boss wants to give you a raise or promotion it's no different to the western world. Provided the relevant internal parties have agreed on the details it's all forwarded to HR and a done deal. Unless of course there's a Qatari who wants the same role...

According to local laws, at least 20% of a company's workforce should be Qatari.

This rarely happens, and we'll discuss why in the next section, but this arbitrary quota can have all sorts of implications on your pay and promotions.

The most common scenario is that a local Qatari gets promoted at lightening speed and at the expense of everyone else. Companies do this because a strong local presence at the executive level can help them win tenders, expand business opportunities and keep the government off their back when they (almost invariably) fail to meet the 20% quota.

It also means your promotion and pay cheque are dependent on no other Qatari wanting the job in question.

Promotions in the Government Sector

Promotions and pay rises in the government sector are a study in bored indifference. Firstly, there's no such thing as a 'career path' for expats. It's not uncommon to hear stories of people who haven't seen a promotion or pay rise in several years.

In most cases, the only way to secure a promotion is to transfer to a new department or an entirely new organisation. Not surprisingly, this tends to play havoc with staff retention rates.

If you accept a role with a government organisation in Qatar be prepared for the fact that your salary is unlikely to increase for the duration of your employment. Meanwhile, inflation rates of around 3.5% per annum mean your salary actually decreases year on year. It's little wonder that most people up and leave after about three years.

About that Pay Rise

A prominent government organisation in Qatar was notorious for the rivalry between its head office and satellite departments. Directors would regularly try and poach staff from each other and even sabotage projects. This worked in the expat's favour since it was the only way to secure a promotion and pay rise.

The problem was that even securing a promotion didn't automatically mean you received the associated pay rise. Getting the extra money signed off by the CEO and down to HR could easily take 12 months. And then you'd be told they needed new copies of your entire employment history. This meant original signed letters from every former boss stamped by both your embassy AND the Qatari Ministry of Foreign Affairs.

If you were super cynical you might think the company didn't want to give you any extra money.

Qatarisation

Qatarisation is an official government policy designed to increase the number of Qataris in all joint venture organisations and government departments. Officially, 20% of a company's employees should be Qatari. This jumps to 50% in the public sector.

Here's the thing, the country gets very nervous about having so many foreigners in the workforce. To offset this, and keep the local population happy, Qatarisation actively favours and fast tracks Qataris when it comes to jobs and careers. Its long-term goal is to ensure that all major companies and organisations are run by Qataris.

In theory, this makes perfect sense. In reality, not so much...

The haste with which Qataris are promoted (especially in the private sector), means you'll often encounter situations where someone with no practical expertise is leap-frogged to managerial level almost immediately. This has a knock-on effect, and means the next local to graduate also expects to go straight into a managerial role as well.

What you end up with is a huddle of local directors and managers, completely out of their depth, being propped up by western consultants. These expats have been brought over to ensure the whole enterprise doesn't keel over in a flurry of long corporate lunches and InShaAllahs.

All well and good, except the people behind the scenes soon realise they're stuck doing the legwork with no prospect of a promotion or even a pay rise.

The high turnover rates associated with expats (2-3 years max) can be at least partly attributed to this lack of career progression. There's also the work related issues that come about when managers with no experience are set loose to terrorise day-to-day operations.

Moving on… The relatively high wages and short working hours within government organisations make them a preferred destination for many Qataris. But for those with ambition and drive, the private sector is the quickest way to climb the corporate ladder. The lack of competition from other nationals and the Qatari quotas means a halfway-competent local will find themselves promoted at speed.

Behaviour Clauses

Most companies don't have any behaviour clauses outside the usual stuff you'd expect back home, i.e. gross negligence, sexual harassment, etc. The obvious exception to this is Qatar Airways.

Flight attendants (read: young women) that take a job with the airline are bound by strict clauses that affect every facet of day-to-day life. This includes getting work to 'okay' your marriage, and having to report a pregnancy as soon as you find out (so the company can fire you).

While those two are perennial favourites amongst outraged western newspapers and human rights organisations, they're simply the peak of a very spiky pyramid.

Without going into a whole spiel about this, female flight staff can expect to live in a residential tower where their departure and arrival is strictly monitored. They are required to be back in their building at least 10 hours before a flight, and have curfews in place even when 'on the ground'. They are not allowed to have guests over after a certain hour, and are definitely not allowed to have men back to their apartments.

In other words, you can expect to forfeit your western liberties if you take a job with Qatar Airways. And while they're the most obvious culprit, they're certainly not the only one. So make sure you read the fine print before accepting an offer, because behaviour that wouldn't raise an eyebrow in the west can get your fired in a heartbeat out in the Gulf.

You're Fired #1

[Name redacted] worked for a government organisation and was supplied her own three-bedroom apartment as part of her package. Being European and weird like that, she decided to rent out the spare rooms via AirBnB. When her work was made aware of this she was fired on the spot and put on a plane home. As far as her work was concerned, allowing strange men to rent a room in your apartment was no different to prostitution.

Your Fired #2

A female Qatar Airways employee was found passed out outside the gate to her compound in the middle of the night. This made international news when a senior executive at the airline sent a CCTV screen grab of the incident to staff as an example of how 'not to conduct yourself'. Whether the girl was drunk, drugged, or some combination of the above was never established, but she was promptly let go.

---Office Politics---

Bad Drama and Heat Madness

Qatar offers a unique work environment for the western expat. It's the sort of country where qualified professionals are in such short supply you can find yourself promoted into a managerial position simply because you're the last person standing.

If you have the stomach to deal with all the petty rivalries, inter-departmental sabotage and screaming meltdowns that characterise day-to-day work life, you can quickly climb the corporate ladder.

Indeed, one of the country's biggest drawcards is the fact you can cram several years worth of promotions and corporate grinding into a handful of summers. By the time you feel dead on the inside and ready to catch the next flight out, you'll have leap-frogged your colleagues back home and have a LinkedIn profile that suggests far more experience than you actually have. You may also have a serious drinking problem, but that's another story.

The point is, you need to stick it out for a few years in order to reap the rewards. And that's easier said than done when your office staff comprise a lot of undiagnosed mental patients.

Granted, office politics are a factor in any company, but Qatar has elevated petty workplace dramas to explosive new heights. This can be attributed to a number of factors including:

- Heat madness
- Impossible to navigate bureaucracy
- A melting point of divergent cultures
- The general stress of completing even the simplest tasks.

All the above creates a powder keg atmosphere that can be set off at any time by the most innocuous events. But here's the rub: Normal, well-adjusted people don't usually relocate to the middle of the desert. It takes a certain kind of disposition to end up out here.

Someone once told me that everyone in Qatar is either running away from or running towards something. Whatever it is they're doing, most of them seem incapable of achieving it without screaming at colleagues, bursting into tears, becoming obsessively territorial, trying to fuck over random people and ultimately suffering a complete mental breakdown.

How to Survive the Workplace

Don't trust anyone
The typical Qatari office has more political intrigue than a season of *Game of Thrones*. The higher you rise the more you'll have to deal with territorial department heads that feel any success you achieve is a reflection of their own failures. This is further heightened by the cultural tensions (and respective work ethics) of expats and Qataris.

This creates a siege mentality where everyone is constantly looking over their shoulders and trying to protect their own interests while keeping the competition, i.e. their co-workers, in their place.

One prominent government organisation in Qatar had a Chief Marketing Officer who was infamous for going on long rants about co-workers in meetings. Seemingly unable to censor herself, she would bitch and moan about whoever wasn't present. Of course word got back to these people, and everyone soon realised that she was slagging off her entire department (and other departments) behind their back. And then the resignations started flooding in…

When a branding consultant was brought in to assist the same organisation, he quickly decided he didn't like two senior people on the team. Within three months of his arrival both members had left the organisation. But not before several shouting matches inside a not very well insulated office. And if it makes you feel any better, he was eventually fired by the same Chief Marketing Officer, who was also slagging him off behind his back.

Sure, this kind of thing happens throughout the world, but Qatar doesn't offer you the luxury of a competent HR department or internal mediation. Which means any workplace conflict becomes a war of attrition until someone leaves.

Make alliances

Because of all this rivalry and back stabbing, it's important to have friends in your corner. What you really need is a handful of people scattered throughout the organisation that are privy to inside information. If you do it right you'll be able to piece together the tid-bits of information from various departments into a more complete picture of what's actually going on at the organisation.

This will not only keep you updated with internal gossip, you'll know when that new apartment complex is going to be taking on staff members. Or when the organisation has squandered all its money on an ill-advised film festival and will have to cut one-third of its workforce.

Keep your mouth shut

The important thing about internal gossip and secrets is knowing when to utilise them. If you want people to keep telling you things they have to believe you can keep your mouth shut. Office secrets are like building a stock portfolio, you try and acquire as much as you can. And while you gotta let a couple go here and there, you want to hold on to that nest egg until the opportune time. That may mean a new vacancy that's (secretly) opened up, or fending off the corporate lawyers when you leave the country unannounced with the company domain names still legally yours.

Naturally, you're going to have to give up some information in return for what you're getting. But it's all about playing the long game. A regular drip feed of information to your friends will keep them happy and will keep the information flowing back to you. Just don't get drunk at a party and tell everyone everything…

Do your job

Ideally, you want to do your job well, ignore all the office drama and get on with your life. Anywhere else in the world, those are desirable traits that should keep you gainfully employed. The problem is it's stupidly difficult to accomplish even the simplest of tasks in Qatar. A combination of nightmarish bureaucracy and incompetence means you're constantly at the mercy of others.

Firstly, your co-workers do not necessarily share your sense of urgency. Qatari employees in government departments are notorious for leaving the office at 2pm (if not earlier) and not giving a single fuck about that thing that 'has to be finished'. Because obviously 'InShaAllah'.

Also, suppliers are notoriously unreliable throughout the region. Whether it's Lactose-free milk from a major supermarket chain or the right paper stock for a brochure, you're entirely at the mercy of some guy who doesn't care if you live or die.

It is therefore important to choose your projects wisely. Anything that involves more than a handful of people should be palmed off to someone else at the first opportunity. At the very least, try and ensure you're not the one responsible for getting that ridiculous / nightmarish / ill-conceived project completed on time. If you have an MBA to your name you should already know how to do this, for everyone else, here are my suggstions:

1.

Find a bored or under-utilised employee and tell them you'd like them to 'take ownership' of this project. Suggest that this is their moment to shine, that you have the utmost confidence in their ability and will give them complete autonomy to complete 'the thing' however they see fit.

Two important notes:

i. The 'take ownership' approach only works with western expats who have grown up within a capitalist framework of individuality, personal responsibility and getting ahead. Your typical Qatari will have no desire to take on any unnecessary responsibility and will simply ignore the task / request.

ii. Make sure you're not going to be held accountable for the outcome of said project. The whole point of farming out a project is to make sure your fingerprints aren't on the impending train crash.

2.

Kill the project before it gets off the ground.

Qatari corporations have short attention spans. If you can delay a project for long enough there's a good chance it will get swept away in a torrent of resignations, firings, 'refocusing' or general disinterest.

Long research undertakings are a great way to drag out the start of any project. A ridiculous budget request will also halt an impending project. Even in Qatar, corporations have to pretend they care about money. And if all else fails, you can try and blame cultural sensitivities.

Always Have a Back-Up Plan

Things could change out here at the drop of hat. Since there's no democracy, parliament or anything resembling a series of 'checks and balances', all it takes is a royal decree and your entire organisation could be out of business. Or the price of oil might plummet and the entire expat staff could be sent home.

Point is, you should have a back-up plan, and take certain precautions to ensure you're not stuck in the country with large debts and no job. A few basic tips:

1. Stash your money away in offshore accounts. If you are fired or made redundant your employer/sponsor can freeze your local bank account while they sort out the paperwork, figure out how much you owe in personal loans and all the rest of it. You don't want to be in that position.
2. Don't take out huge loans. If you resign from your job or are made redundant you'll need to pay back all your loans and suchlike before you're granted permission to leave the country. If that happens much sooner than you anticipate, you may find yourself with a fancy new car that you need to sell fast and at way below market value — leaving you with a sizeable bill to clear before you can fly out.
3. Realise that your time in Qatar is limited and is unlikely to last much longer than three or four years, max. Think about what you want to do after and start laying the groundwork for a job post-Qatar. If you're planning to head home accept that your next job is unlikely to include the same perks you've enjoyed in the desert.

4. Have your passport and credit card nearby. In a worst-case scenario you want to be at the airport and on the next flight out within an hour. Not to say that's ever going to happen, but it's better to be safe than stuck in Qatar.

---Advice for the Newly Arrived---

Quick Answers to Basic Questions

Can I drink alcohol in Qatar?
The short answer is 'yes'. But there are restrictions. You can drink booze in five-star hotels and their associated restaurants, bars and clubs. You can also drink in the privacy of your own home, but to purchase alcohol for home consumption you'll need a special 'alcohol license' which your employer must approve. They're not under any obligation to do so.

What about sex?
Technically, it's illegal to have sex outside marriage. But it's one of those laws that everyone is happy to ignore. The only time this may become an issue is if a western man has a relationship with a Qatari woman (and her family find out). This is not a situation you want to find yourself in... Also, if you're planning on giving birth in Qatar you'll need to supply the father's name. If he's not your husband you can face jail time and deportation. All of this depends on your passport, surname, etc, but we'll get into all that later in the book.

Is the country safe?

Yes, very much so. Forget what Fox News has told you, the Middle East is not all religion and violence. Qatar is one of the safest countries in the world, with a very low crime rate. Or to put it another way, you're more likely to be assaulted, robbed, or murdered in the U.S., U.K., or Australia.

Do I need Arabic language skills?

No, you'll be totally fine with English. While Arabic is the official language, almost everyone speaks some English, and most Qataris are fluid in conversational English. Knowing some Arabic can help you when it comes to negotiating deals or bartering at the markets, but menus, road signs and almost everything else is in both Arabic and English.

Can I come and go as I please?

That depends. If you're over on a tourist visa and doing 'Dubai runs' while working off-the-books you can come and go as you please. If you're over officially then you'll have a sponsor and they can dictate the terms of your coming and going.

Will I be sexually harassed?

If you're a woman, the honest answer is 'almost certainly'. Whether it's construction workers from South Asia or local guys in LandCruisers, attitudes towards women are a little different out here. Harassment is an unfortunate fact of life.

Will I earn a fortune and retire rich?
Depends. Life in Qatar is surprisingly expensive for westerners, and it's very easy to waste the bulk of your pay on rent, fancy hotels, cars, holidays and the sort of lifestyle that this place encourages. If you want to earn serious money you'll need to work in the construction or oil industry for a private company. Government-associated jobs have much lower pay grades for foreigners, but they usually include accommodation and various other perks.

Should I come to Qatar?
That's up to you. If you're adventurous, open minded and halfway competent at what you do, then Qatar offers all kinds of opportunities. Just don't stay for more than 3-4 years.

Making Friends is Easy

Making friends in Qatar is easy because virtually everyone is new in town and looking to meet people. Back home, you would have cultivated a circle of friends throughout high school, university, work and whatever. Those roots don't exist in the desert, so you're forced to start over.

The goods news is people are hiring and they're not that fussy. Talk to someone who's been out here longer than you, and they'll almost certainly invite you out to a house party or drinks thing. Say 'yes' to all these invites and you'll quickly find yourself surrounded by a posse of raging alcoholics and degenerate fuck-ups.

Meeting people is easy. Meeting people you actually want to hang out with (while sober) is a lot trickier. Initially, you'll just want something to do and someone to do it with, so you won't be that fussed about the people you're hanging with. That's fine. But there may come a point where you look around and realise you hate your entire social circle.

This epiphany can strike at any time. It can happen while picking up the drinks tab at a shitty nightclub, while watching creepy old guys hit on girls at an after party or while having dinner with bunch of boring assholes at some restaurant that doesn't serve alcohol.

Whatever the scenario, there will be a point where you realise 'these are not my people', and start culling left, right and centre.

This is actually totally normal and healthy. There's nothing more depressing than going out with people you have nothing in common with, laughing awkwardly at their racist jokes, and watching them bemoan the laziness of their Filipino staff — which they have woken at 3am to make you a cocktail.

And if You Get Desperate…

Any city with a large expat community will have professional 'social groups', i.e. InterNations and the like. They're a chance for strangers to come together in a desperate attempt to make conversation and/or unplanned babies.

Thanks to the miracle of Facebook algorithms, you'll probably see paid ads for these groups cropping up in your news feed soon after your arrival. They will usually feature a selection of good-looking people (of various ethnicities) standing around with drinks in hand, obviously having the time of their life.

There's nothing wrong with attending one of these things. If you genuinely enjoy meeting people and think geographic location is the basis of a lasting friendship, they're a quick fix for dull weekends. But they're also pretty straight laced.

Due to their open nature, these societies tend to attract the full spectrum of expats. So what you end up with is a bunch of 40-year-old business guys, random nerds and crazy girls who post passive-aggressive messages on social media, all having an alcohol-free dinner at a local Yemenese restaurant.

While this is fascinating from an anthropological perspective, it's a world away from the glamour portrayed in the promotional ads.

Becoming Official (the Dreaded Medical)

Part 1. Do I have a terrible disease?

The sooner you get yourself a residency card the better. It means you no longer have to drag out your passport to get into bars, and it makes the mundane tasks associated with moving country (phone plans, apartment rental, etc.), a lot easier.

Before being granted residency you need to undergo a full medical exam. The exam consists of a blood test, a chest x-ray and a general once-over by a doctor. Basically, they want to ensure you don't have AIDs or tuberculosis, both of which mean instant deportation.

Whether or not they also test for drugs is never clarified, but this is the Gulf, so you'd be advised to make sure your system is 'clean' before heading over. As a basic guide, marijuana traces can show up in your system for up to a month. Pills, coke and suchlike have a much shorter half-life, and should be gone within 4-5 days. If you're in doubt, there's a flourishing online trade in 'system cleansing kits'.

But here's the thing; there's only one medical facility dedicated to testing expats, and it's desperately understaffed. It can take a month or longer before anyone from your company remembers that you need a medical and manages to book an appointment. So theoretically, you can get bombed on mind altering drugs right up until you board your flight to Qatar (if you're into that kind thing), and still pass whatever blood tests they have planned for you.

The downside is you'll be tested at the exact same facilities as all the construction workers from South East Asia. Whether you're a highly paid executive or a labourer from Pakistan, you're going to get shuffled through the same corridors, same machines and exam rooms. If your experiences in Qatar have been limited to five-star hotels and cocktail lounges it can be quite a culture shock to suddenly find yourself lumped in with all the 'slave labourers' you've read about in *The Guardian*.

Part 2. The actual medical process

Once a date and time has been scheduled, a 'minder' from your company will drive you (and any other new employees), out to the medical facility for your miscellaneous tests.

What's supposed to happen is you walk into a large shed-like waiting area, a man at a battered looking desk will inspect your passport, type up a document (on an equally battered typewriter), attach your photo and point you towards a doctor.

The reality is a little different. Government employees in the Gulf can be somewhat relaxed, so it's not unusual to arrive and find typewriter guy has disappeared for a couple of hours. Since you can't do anything else until he processes your form you just have to sit there and wait. In order to make this extra weird, they have a special 'VIP' waiting area for western professionals — essentially, a handful of seats that face 400 South Asian workers crammed in a paddock.

While you sit there and read your book (make sure you bring something to read!), truckloads of labourers will arrive at the same facility and take their designated seats opposite you, starring intently at any western woman who may be around. If you're a western woman you will (hopefully) be getting used to the starring.

At some point you may be tempted to pull out your phone and start taking photos of all this — between the South Asians in the paddocks, the faded posters from the 1980s, the vintage typewriter and the general low-rent ambiance of the place, it could pass for a Tate Modern art installation about post-colonialism.

Please resist that urge. No one appreciates a tourist and it's very hard to take a photo of someone's ramshackle desk in the Middle East without rousing Edward Said from his coffin. But that's a whole other book...

Part 3. Put a needle in me I'm done

Once the typewriter guy returns there will be a mad scramble to get his attention. This is when you need to have your minder nearby. He'll already have 'an arrangement' in place, and will push you to the front of the queue where you will be processed ahead of everyone else. Get used to it. The next few hours will see you being ushered past lines of brown skinned workers while your guy yells "VIP" and drags you around by the collar.

The technical aspects of the blood test and chest x-ray aren't really worth getting into. The actual medical facility (across from the holding shed) is reasonably clean and modern. The guy who takes your blood uses a new syringe for every person and can find veins with the competence that comes from doing the same thing several hundred times a day, every day.

The chest x-ray will have you removing your shirt and standing in line with a group of labourers until you're ushered into a room and pressed up against the machines. The same machine that hundreds of other naked men have been pushed up against all day. If you're weird about germs, this would be a good day to take some valium or whatever you use to kill any 'feels'.

Incidentally, there's a separate women's area where all these same tests take place and you're provided with the relevant medical garb. It's a lot less busy than the men's side. Probably because women are smarter than men and know to avoid the Gulf…

All up, you're looking at about four hours hanging out at this medical centre, being ushered around, poked and prodded. When the whole thing is over you'll be wanting to get your drink on.

Easy Credit and Free Money

Qatar may be one of the wealthiest countries in the world, but the local population is heavily in debt. This is because Qataris like to buy Ferraris, stay in five-star hotels and travel first class. And they do all of this on cheap credit cards and very generous bank loans.

That kind of reckless spending can be infectious and local financial institutions are happy to oblige western expats with cheap loans. If you've ever wanted to get yourself dangerously in debt, this is the country.

Most of the major companies (and all the government departments) have established relationships with one of the major banks. A representative from said bank will usually be in contact within a week of your arrival to set up your account and give you a credit card. And they REALLY want you to take that credit card. They'll even visit you at your work desk with the paper work.

Regardless of your credit history, the banks will give you around USD $6000 (20,000 QR) in credit without batting an eyelid. They'll also happily spring for a car loan. Again, this varies according to organisation, but a government job should provide around USD $15,000 (50,000 QR) interest-free to purchase a car. Of course if you want to buy a Ferrari (or several LandCruisers), the banks have got your back, but you'll have to pay some nominal interest.

And therein lies the pitfall. Although the banks will lend you stupid amounts of money and ask virtually zero questions, you can't leave the country until it's paid back in full. So if you take out a USD $150,000 loan for a Mercedes G Wagon you'll want to ensure your job security is up to par — or you have someone who can sneak you out of the country if worst comes to worst.

The Three-Month Crisis

Your first couple of months in the Gulf will be surreal. If you're anything like the typical western expat, you'll have found yourself giving up a 'comfortable' apartment and public transport in favour of a five-star hotel suite and having a driver chauffer you to work.

You will #humblebrag about this on social media, even as you try and get you're your head around this strange new life you're inhabiting. Whatever your expectations may have been, watching the sun dip over the desert horizon as the evening call to prayer rings out, is an amazing scene. At least for the first couple of weeks…

Around the three-month point things will have settled into a routine. Your work probation will be drawing to an end, and you'll probably be looking at purchasing a car and moving into long-term accommodation. All of a sudden the Gulf isn't some abstract adventure, but your reality for the next couple of years.

The other thing you'll start to realise around the three-month mark is that contact with your old friends back home will have significantly diminished. While your Facebook messages back home were initially met with enthusiastic replies, those same messages are now starting to go unanswered. Text messages to friends are disappearing into a void, Skype dates are getting harder to organise and you start to feel that people are maybe forgetting about you.

All of this can be magnified by feelings of isolation, bouts of depression and those mornings where you wake up and wonder what the hell you're doing in the middle of the desert.

As the weeks and months progress and you don't hear back from people, you'll begin to realise that the move overseas has also meant the end of several friendships. This can be tough to deal with, and it's not uncommon to find yourself spiralling into various shades of melancholy.

Before you know it, you'll be scrolling through photos of your exes on Facebook, falling into Fleetwood Mac playlists on YouTube, sleeping with people you'd ignore under normal circumstances and eating entire tubs of ice cream from your fancy hotel bed.

The thing is, your friends back home will be oblivious to this. They've got their own lives to live, people to see and problems to deal with. To them you've become an abstraction; a Facebook feed of exotic photos, strange stories and updates about dust storms. They assume you're having the time of your life and don't realise just how important those calls, messages and Skype sessions are.

In the meantime there's not much point catching emotions or getting depressed. Accept your new life, think of the experiences you're accruing and go out and meet people. You didn't travel to the other side of the world to sit in a hotel room and watch MTV.

I Need My Drugs

Self-medication is an elaborate cocktail that everyone has to work out for themselves. Uppers, downers, screamers, laughers; whatever helps you get through the night. The good news is you can source most of the classic ingredients easily enough in Qatar.

Before setting out for Qatar I stocked up on months of cold 'n' flu tablets (the proper kind), and made my local GP write me a script saying I needed the pseudoephedrine contained within to stop me from dying. Even then, I was a little nervous as I went through customs that first time.

I shouldn't have worried. Despite the horror stories you may have heard about Dubai travellers getting arrested for poppy-seed bagels, the Gulf has a surprisingly relaxed attitude to prescription drugs. You can purchase things like cold 'n' flu tablets (the real kind) without any sort of script. Meanwhile, Viagra, diet pills, anxiety stuff and more can be readily acquired at most pharmacies, but you'll need to get a local doctor's script.

Since you won't know any local doctors when you first arrive, or anything else about the country, it's a good idea to stock up beforehand. Go see your local GP back home, explain that you're going overseas and have them pre-emptively diagnose you for every disease and scenario that springs to mind.

Do you suffer from bad nerves, narcolepsy or steroid addiction? Not sure? Best to get some drugs prescribed just in case. Concerned the desert heat may cause performance anxiety? Maybe get yourself a Viagra prescription. Continue down this road until you have a suitcase full of drugs, and enough scripts to emerge alive and fully erect from an Ebola outbreak...

While this should keep you alive for the first few months, at some point your homegrown stash will deplete, and you'll be forced to re-up. Here's the thing; drug classifications vary wildly around the world, and while certain prescriptions meds are easily obtainable in Qatar, others do require a local GP's hand-written note.

Anxiety drugs, uppers, 'erectile dysfunction' meds and suchlike, will, unfortunately, require a visit to a local GP. And look, for what's it worth, the local medical service isn't bad. As long as you have private insurance and avoid the main hospitals Qatar it's pretty good at keeping people alive. It's just, you know, boring and weird seeing a doctor in a foreign country.

If you're desperate (and don't want to see a local doctor for whatever reason) you can always try your luck with some back-alley pharmacies and your scripts from back home. Like most things in Qatar, there are official rules and then there's the local 'interpretations'.

Or if that isn't clear enough, certain pharmacists will sell you whatever you ask for, whether or not you have the required local script. Or any script...

Getting drugs without a script
I thought that the more shoddy and rundown the pharmacy, the more likely they'd ignore the rules and sell me Xanax. But I quickly

realised that the ghetto outlets weren't much use. For starters, they're pretty badly stocked, so most times they didn't have anything good. Or worse, you'd find a pair of old ninjas (women in abayas and a hijab) behind the counter, and they would just judge the shit out of you while talking to each other in Arabic. Eventually, a nice shiny place in one of the local malls helped out. They said my script from overseas wasn't valid, but they sold it to me when I made sad puppy dog eyes and asked if "there was anything else they could do".

Phillip – Germany. Project manager.

Section 3. Dating, Romance, and a Social Life

---Drinking & Partying in the Desert---

A Beginner's Guide

For a Muslim country with an extremely dim view of public drunkenness, Qatar can be a surprisingly boozy place. Fact is, you'll probably find yourself drinking more than you did back home. This isn't some strange coincidence. This country leads you to drink.

Before we get into all that, it's worth noting that the only 'officially sanctioned' places you can get hammered on Long Islands and suchlike, are hotel bars and private residences. As far as the authorities are concerned, luxury hotels are neutral zones where local customs don't apply and charging USD $20 for a beer is a reasonable thing to do.

Any religious concerns about selling booze in a Muslim country are offset by the TRUCKLOADS of money it brings in. Also, it allows westerners to forget that they're in the middle of a desert. But more on that later…

See you in hell

The Qur'an forbids the consumption of alcohol by Muslims. Heathen infidels, i.e. Western Christians, get a pass because they're going to hell anyway, so it makes no difference. Drinking Too Much in Doha

If you don't have a drinking problem when you first arrive in Qatar, don't worry, you'll soon develop one.

Just like the British colonialists that menaced the region over the last couple of centuries, the modern expat spends a lot of their time either drunk or recovering from drinking.

Let's call it a 'copying mechanism'. Booze nulls the pain at the end of the working week… Or the start. And the subsequent hangover means you're too woozy to think about anything besides food and self-loathing.

Medical professionals will throw around words like 'alcoholism' to describe this behaviour. Pour yourself another drink and ignore them. The key to surviving life in Qatar is to keep yourself just drunk enough to ignore the fact you're actually in Qatar. This is why there's such a big mid-week party scene.

Back home in the west the heavy drinking is generally reserved for weekends. Qatar expats will be lucky to make it past Tuesday morning without a hangover. And there's no shortage of dodgy clubs and hotel bars to assist you with the above.

Of course the longer you stay in the country the harder it is to walk that fine line between 'let's get drunk' and 'I have a serious drinking problem and should probably seek professional help'. But what's life without challenges?

The Bottle Shop

Any expat that's been in Qatar longer than five minutes will eagerly point out that there is only one bottle shop to service the entire country. They will then either shrug, sigh, roll their eyes, or some combination of the three. The lack of bottle shop options is a running joke. It's just not a particularly funny one.

Oh, and it gets worse. You can't just walk into the bottle shop and buy alcohol like a normal person. You need to get a 'liquor license' first. And that requires an official 'okay' from your employer.

It breaks down like this: any expat making over a certain amount of money (i.e. anyone reading this), can get an official letter from their work enabling them to buy booze. It's supposed to be a formality. But nothing is ever that easy in Qatar.

Firstly, the consumption of alcohol is still seen as a social taboo in Qatar. So even if you're a white guy named Chet who grew up in New Jersey and has no religious affiliation, the locals are going to silently judge your application for a license.

Getting the paperwork sorted isn't THAT difficult, you just need to be aware that employers keep track of who's applied. This can make things awkward for anyone who looks like they might be from the Middle East or has Mohammed anywhere in their name. And while a company can't legally prevent you from getting a license on religious grounds, it takes a devil-may-care attitude to apply for one as a Muslim in Qatar.

Also, some employers have a blanket policy that forbids their staff from purchasing alcohol, i.e. Qatar Airways cabin crew. These poor bastards have to live with a whole lot of restrictions on what they can and can't do. They deal with this by getting wasted on the alcohol their friends secretly buy for them.

But we're getting sidetracked… The bottle shop is known as Qatar Distribution Centre (QDC for short) and is located out in the middle of nowhere. There's a monthly limit on how much booze you can purchase (based on your income), but unless you're a raging alcoholic it should be ample to keep you buzzed and help out a few people.

Also, since no one can be bothered with the hellish commute out to the shop, most people will buy in bulk when they're forced to restock. Spending a lazy USD $1000 on one of these trips is absolutely normal.

Back in 2012 a second, much more conveniently located, QDC branch was opened at The Pearl. Despite the lengthy approval process that the owners went through, the shop lasted half a day before someone in power had it shut down. It was never spoken of again…

Overpriced Booze and Pork Products

Alcohol at the QDC bottle shop is expensive. Not as ridiculous as the price gouging that goes on at the hotels, but you can still expect to pay around USD $50   for a bottle of brand-name spirit. There are also weird imported options from India, and while they're considerably cheaper, a Bombay Rum hangover is a special kind of hell.

Still, there's a decent selection of booze on offer. All the usual top-shelf spirits are available and they have wine and champagne options from around the world.

They also have pork! The QDC bottle shop is the one place in Qatar where you can legally buy 'proper' bacon and an assortment of swine-filled deli goods. Of course it's all been imported and frozen for weeks, so you're not going to get that exotic miracle ham you might be used to back home, but it's a start.

Oh, and speaking of pork laws, Qatar customs have their very own passport stamp for those who try and bring some Spanish chorizos or whatever back into the country. Get busted smuggling pork and not only will they confiscate it, they'll stamp your passport with a special 'pork smuggler' stamp*. Which, when you think about it, is actually kind of awesome, and almost reason enough to start an exciting new career putting bratwurst down your pants.

*I've never been able to verify the pork smuggler story. But let's run with it.

Qataris Buying Booze

Qataris aren't legally permitted to buy booze from the QDC because of the whole 'Muslim thing', but they have a pretty solid work-around. They'll assign a liquor license to one of their low-level employees, e.g. the driver, and inflate their salary on the paperwork. These guys will then go out to the QDC and buy the booze on behalf of their Qatari employers. It's simple, terrible and effective.

Bars, Clubs, Drinks, Cocktails

Having a social life in Doha means hanging out in luxury hotel bars. That's because only five-star hotels are allowed to serve booze.

Qatar's whole relationship with alcohol is actually pretty weird, but we don't have time to get into it here. Suffice to say, serving booze in luxury hotels is a compromise that keeps everyone reasonably happy. It also means all the decent bars, clubs and restaurants are located within said hotels.

You can ignore all this and spend your time doing 'authentic' things like hanging out at the Souq, going camping in the desert, or parking outside Turkish restaurants in a 4WD and aggressively honking your horn until someone comes out with a Shawarma, but those activities are all lame and boring after you've done them once.

So that leaves hotels bars and their overpriced drinks. Which is what you're going to spend the bulk of your free time doing. Before you know it, you'll be well acquainted with the subtle nuisances of Beach Party Fridays, Sunday Ladies Night, Tuesday R&B Nights, and how to sneak into the poolside bar at the Sheraton on weekday afternoons.

You'll also become an expert at spotting Romanian hookers, showing up at work on four hours sleep and logging out of your social media accounts ahead of time, so you don't post anything that might potentially get you fired.

While this is all fun and games to begin with, the novelty will inevitably wear thin. Clubs like Crystal at the W are a fun distraction until you look around and realise you're surrounded by the worst kind of human scum 'popping bottles in the VIP'.

Also, the soundtrack is nothing but 'club remixes' of Chris Brown tracks. So really, the tequila shots are there to stop you from killing yourself…

I'd buy that for a dollar

Skip to the end of the book for a comprehensive guide to Filipino hooker bars, drunken Saudis hangouts, terrible Lebanese nightclubs, and old school hotel lounges.

Valet Parking

Unless you're legitimately wealthy, you probably don't make a habit of valet parking in the west. But then you probably don't spend your weekends hanging out in five-star hotels either.

As previously discussed, Doha's entire nightlife is centered around the W Hotel, the Hilton and whatever the latest addition is. Since there's no public transport (and who catches a bus to a five-star hotel anyway?), your options are to either call a private driver or take a car.

Really, you should probably just take a private driver as they're dirt cheap, readily available, and ensure you won't get deported for driving through someone's house while blind drunk. If you don't have a regular guy you can always just Uber it.

All fine and good, but sometimes you're going to find yourself in a position where you have to pull up to a hotel and hand your keys to a man in a vest. There's a subtle etiquette to this.

First up, all the valet people in Doha are polite enough to ignore the 'no drink driving' laws. You could fall out of your car while laughing manically, but as long as you're not clutching a bottle of Patron and trying to fight the hotel staff with it, everyone will avert their eyes.

The same rule applies at closing time. Everyone spills out of the hotels at 2:30am drunkenly waving their ticket stubs at the valets. Since nobody wants to cause a scene they simply push the patrons into their Lambos, Beamers and whatever else they're driving.

Oh yeah, tipping! Okay, so it's not mandatory to tip the staff, but when you're paying more per drink then they make in several hours you should throw them some change before you drunkenly veer off into traffic.

While there's no hard and fast rule about the going rate for valet parking, 10 QR will keep everyone happy. It translates to about USD $2.50. To put that in perspective, you're paying around USD $20 (70 QR) per drink at some of these hotels. Long story short; don't be an asshole, tip the valet.

Doha Beach Parties

Spring in Doha is beach party season. The various five-star hotels around town will throw back-to-back-to-back parties for weeks. While the venue and the headliners may change, the parties themselves are virtually interchangeable. They're a fun — but ultimately soul-crushing — mix of vodka Red Bulls, Swedish House Mafia and failed hook-ups. Also, all of the following:

- Headlining has-been DJ from the 90s

- Person attempting to drink the 1-litre canister of vodka and Red Bull by themselves

- Same person vomiting up vodka and Red Bull

- Old gross guy with two Filipino hookers

- People going crazy to the latest piece of shit from Swedish House Mafia

- Local DJ playing the same 20 songs that everyone else plays

- Local MC rapping about growing up in the hood

- Dude-bro with no shirt hitting on a random drunk girl

- Someone getting punched in the face for saying hi to a Lebanese girl

- A fight in the queue for the men's toilet

- A couple arguing in public

- Qatari women with fake IDs and no abaya

Secret Abayas at Dance Parties

One fun game you can play at Doha Beach Parties is 'spot the abaya'. The aim is the scan the room and guess which women are Qatari nationals with fake IDs.

I was introduced to this exciting game by a random drunk woman at one of these events. In between taking swigs from her giant canister of vodka and Red Bull, she explained that many younger Qatari women (banned from entering licensed premises by law) get fake IDs. She then proceeded to point out these women in the crowd, which she described as 'Secret Abayas'.

I'm still not sure how she was able to spot these women, or how accurate her guesses were, but they all seemed to be very young, very skinny and very beautiful. I contributed to the conversation by pointing out potential date rapists in the crowd.

While there's nothing beyond anecdotal stories to support all this, there's definitely a generation of younger Qatari women who have grown up on western culture and don't appreciate the government's attempts to keep them sober and in abayas.

Since Qataris are mostly above inconvenient local laws, and often have access to large sums of cash, an underground fake ID circuit isn't exactly far fetched. Because, what's the point of watching *Keeping Up with the Kardashians*, rocking Louis Vuitton handbags and not being able to get 'slizzerd' in a club or beach party?

Generally speaking this is harmless fun — unless you're the hapless expat who tries to pick up one of these women...

If Qatari women are sneaking into clubs with fake IDs they're not doing it on their own, and all these 'Secret Abayas' tend to have large posses with them.
Their male friends will NOT appreciate some westerner talking to 'their women', and getting into a fight with a Qatari guy is just about the fastest way to find yourself in jail and deported.

Shame and Regret (at Nikki Beach)

Part 1.

If you want to see middle-aged Arab men hitting on blonde airline stewards then Nikki Beach is the place to be. Located at the far end of The Pearl (the giant man-made island), it's supposed to be a private beach for residents. In reality, it's the daytime compendium to the club scene — a debauched mix of booze, tans and assholes.

Before we get into all that, it's worth noting that the beach is technically private and you're only supposed to be allowed admission if you have a specific swipe card that residents need to apply for. There's a security guard posted at the entrance whose sole job is to check everyone is official and has their ID. Like most things in Doha, the rules and the reality are a little different.

For starters, the security guards are completely ineffectual and terrified of upsetting the wrong person. Generally, they'll let anyone who looks like they might live at The Pearl enter without saying a word, i.e. if you're white, look like an athlete or are a hot girl in a bikini they'll simply wave you through.

Every once in a while there'll be some sort of management imposed crackdown and the security may ask you for your card. You can easily get around this by saying something like, "Yeah, my housemate has it, they'll be here in a moment." As long as you treat the security with bored disinterest they'll let you straight through.

What you DON'T want to do is stop and engage the security in a conversation. They know from past experience that anyone who's paying to live at The Pearl has no time to argue with a lowly security personal. And yes, it is messed up, but that's the way things work in Qatar. Start apologising to the security because you don't have your swipe card on you and they'll immediately get suspicious.

Part 2.

Right, so that should get you onto Nikki Beach. The reason it's so popular is a) it's one of the only free beaches in Doha and b), you can get away with a lot of bullshit you can't anywhere else.

Five-star hotels in Doha have a monopoly on beachside locations and you have to pay exorbitant fees to access them. The only public beach is at Katara, but it's aimed at families and closely watched by the dudes that ensure 'public morality'. So while it might be free, it's also full of screaming children, overweight old men and women in abayas roasting in the sun.

In comparison, Nikki Beach is basically Sodom and Gomorrah, a small strip of ocean and sand where the normal rules of Qatari society don't apply. Head down on a Saturday afternoon and the vibe is not unlike a shitty nightclub, with everyone doing their best to get noticed, get drunk and, maybe, pick up.

The girls are impossibly toned, tanned and well endowed, and the bikinis are a skimpy as anything you'd see back home. Meanwhile, the guys look like professional athletes and will spend hours practicing their football skills or playing volleyball in little more than underwear. All of which is both great eye candy and somewhat intimidating for those who don't live in a gym or model professionally.

All the above will be sound-tracked by several different portable speakers blaring out a demented mix of David Guetta, Chris Brown and whatever else is 'popping in the clubs' that week.

Also, alcohol! Although consuming booze in public is strictly prohibited in Qatar, Nikki Beach is like one of those 'special economic zones' in North Korea where awkward inconsistencies are glossed over. This potent mix of booze and bikinis simmers in the desert sun, and by early afternoon half the crowd are roaring drunk and completely forget they're in Qatar. Which is when the real fun starts.

Watching the social carnage at Nikki Beach is great spectator sport. And the sight of a drug-fuelled, middle-aged Arab bro being rejected by an airline stewardess is as brutal as it is insightful. There's also the socially-retarded guys on jet-skis who seem to think the way to a woman's heart is to launch heavy machinery at her head...

Seriously though, the general vibe at Nikki Beach is not unlike a skeezy nightclub, or Jersey Shore on acid. Except you can actually see all the party fouls in broad daylight and everyone is wearing fewer clothes.

Camping in the Desert

Going camping in Qatar is an expat right of passage. You're not really 'official' until you've been dragged out to the desert by drunk people who have no idea how to operate a 4WD, downed a bottle of vodka while swimming in the inland sea and woken up covered in sand and regret.

While there are organised camping and dune bashing expeditions available you'll want to avoid these. The camping sites they use look like something out of a zombie apocalypse movie. We're talking several haggard tents forming a circular enclosure with some rusted, gaudy coloured tables in the middle, a 'coffee centre' offering instant coffee from a thermos, and a general air of failure and despair. This is not how you want to live your life. Which is why it's best to tag along with some expats who have done this thing before.

One of the most popular camping spots is the aforementioned inland sea. This is located about two hours south of Doha, and is basically a series of dunes and inlets by the water's edge. Also, you'll get some great views of Saudi Arabia as there's only about 500 metres of water separating the two countries at this point. This gives the whole camping, boozing and naked swimming a perverse edge, since they'd probably burn you as a witch for the above activities on the other side of the water. Assuming that's the kind of stuff you're into.

In any case, Sealine is the midway point between Doha and the inland sea. This is where the highway ends, a final convenience store pop ups on the horizon and you have to deflate the tyres on your 4WD to proceed through the dunes.

Speaking of 4WDs, whatever reservations you may have about LandCruisers in the city are quickly dispelled out here in the dunes. There's a reason everyone owns one, and it's because they're almost indestructible in the desert. Conversely, a Range Rover, Porsche Cayenne or Jeep feels distinctly under-equipped and out of place in the desert.

But let's not turn this into some weird segue about cars. As long as you have a functioning 4WD you should be okay with a convoy of friends. While navigating the desert dunes can be daunting for newcomers, the basic rule of thumb is that the ocean will always be on your left hand side as you drive south. Follow that advice and it's fairly difficult to get lost.

Getting bogged is another matter, and you should always travel in a convoy, but that's the kind of boring advice that anyone driving into the desert should already be familiar with. As for the finer points of not killing yourself driving, I'm not much help on that front (having always preferred to drink alcohol while someone else does the driving).

Here are some things that will happen on every camping expedition:

1. Someone will forget their cigarettes (or assume they can buy some at Sealine) and then spend the rest of the trip 'bumming smokes' off other people. If you smoke make sure you take several packets — and buy them in town before you hit the road
2. People will get drunk and naked before running screaming into the water with a bottle of tequila
3. The same drunk people will make regrettable decisions about who they invite into their tent
4. Someone will decide to go for a drunken drive in the middle of the night but won't make it more than 10

metres before hitting a parked vehicle belonging to a friend

5. At least a couple of people won't get their tents up and will pass out in the desert sand
6. There will be a flat tyre, a car will get bogged and the convoy will get lost.

The Infamous Althani Parties

Drinking, drugs and pre-marital sex are all illegal for Qatari nationals. But that doesn't mean people actually adhere to the rules.

The greatest contrast between how Qatar presents itself and what really goes on can be found at the 'Althani parties'. These secret events hosted by the rich kids from the ruling class, are held in secret nightclubs underneath mansions and are awash with cocaine, booze and Moroccan hookers.

Unconfirmed reports have armed police stationed outside the parties to ensure the guests are not bothered (and the dead hookers are disposed of quickly and efficiently). In other words, they're not much different to the sorts of house parties you might find rich Russian kids attending.

And while the drug overdoses, dead hookers and hidden nightclubs are on the more extreme end of the spectrum, a thriving underground social scene definitely exists for rich Qatari kids. These parties are invite-only, have a strict no photos policy and offer plenty of booze. Of course as a western expat, your chances of seeing this are approximately zero.

---Love and Sex in Qatar---

Dating in the Gulf

The one constant about Qatar and other Gulf states is their transient nature. The average expat sticks around for maybe two or three years. Ask long-term residents why they don't go out of their way to befriend new arrivals and a common response is they've seen too many people come and go over the years to become invested in new arrivals. "What's the point if you know they're going to leave?"

This also applies to dating. Because everyone is aware that their time here is limited, friendships and relationships tend to form quicker. So six months of dating in Qatar is the equivalent of about two years back in the west. And tequila shots at the bar count as a first, second and third date.

Point being; dating, romance and love is a little different in the Gulf. If you want to avoid deportation or worse, it's worth remembering where you are and tread carefully.

Sucks to Be a Single Guy

Qatar is a great country for married couples; mostly because the dating options are so grim. Trying to find your 'life partner' out here is kinda like trying to find a Jewish deli. It's an exercise in futility — especially if you're a guy.

The country's dating problems are vast and numerous. And in the interest of anthropological accuracy, we're going to run through them one by one until you're on Facebook stalking your exes and listening to the Smiths.

1. The ratio of men to women is totally broken.

Unlike the western world where the male / female ratio breaks down as roughly 50/50, in Qatar it's 75% men vs. 25% women. So right from the get-go guys are at a considerable disadvantage.

And when you exclude Qatari women, conservative Muslim women from neighbouring countries and low-paid Filipino workers, you're left with about 2-3% of the population. These are not great odds.

2. The whole 'Muslim thing'.

The vast majority of Qatar's population is Muslim. Now obviously they're not a unified block, and views on drinking, dating and sexing vary from individual to individual. But you can pretty much throw your western dating expectations out the window. This isn't Spring Break and you're not in South Beach, Florida.

Common questions you'll find yourself asking as a single man include:

- Are local women allowed to date?
- Are local women allowed to date a westerner?
- Will I get to sex them before marriage?
- Will the family want to kill me?

The short (and not very satisfying) answer to the above is "it varies." While westerns have been brought up to imagine that all Muslims (especially those living in the Gulf) follow the same conservative guidelines, the reality is that people tend to cherry pick the rules that suit them.

Granted, a woman wearing an abaya is unlikely to meet you for a drink at a hotel bar. But even women who assume all the trappings of western culture, including booze and nightclubs, may not date a western infidel such as yourself.

3. The lack of drinking (see also, The whole 'Muslim' thing).

If you're dating in the west then it's pretty much assumed that you're drinking. A few drinks under your belt helps keep the conversation flowing and calms the nerves when you're meeting some random person from Tinder in a local bar.

That's not necessarily going to be the case in Qatar. Even if you do manage to go on a date with a local woman, there's a strong chance she won't drink. And so you end up with scenarios like below…

Do you even party?

I was at nightclub with a friend when we ran into one of her colleagues, Yasmin. Yasmin was in her mid 20s, originally from Singapore and spilling out of her tight green dress. When I offered to buy another round I asked her what she was drinking, and she said "A virgin Bloody Mary." Obviously I asked her "Why virgin?" She explained that Ramadan started in a week and she had stopped drinking alcohol a month in advance for religious reasons....

Martin, Canada, Engineer

That sort of discontinuity happens a lot in Qatar. And it makes navigating the whole dating thing a complete mystery for outsiders.

4. No public displays of affection.

Say you go on a date back in the west; if things are going well you might end up at your favorite bar, in some dimly lit corner booth, knocking back drinks. If there's some chemistry there then one thing might lead to the next and yada, yada... In Doha there are no discrete, dimly lit bars. And even if there were, security would quickly intervene and tell you to knock it off if things got too cosy.

5. So that just leaves other western expats.

Ultimately, you're going to be reduced to a very small pool of western expat women which you have a legitimate shot at dating. And since every other guy in Qatar is going to be throwing themselves at these same women, you've got to bring something substantial to the table if you want to stand out.

This is difficult when you find yourself in a bar or club surrounded by professional athletes shipped in from overseas and seriously rich local dudes with a Ferrari parked outside.

Sad stories about failed dates

I met Nadia at a friend's birthday drinks. We were all hanging out in a bar knocking back cocktails while Nadia stuck with coke — as in cola. When I asked her about this she said that she hadn't touched alcohol for two years as she used to be 'out of control'. Anyway, we ended up exchanging contact details at the end of the night and a week later we meet up for a coffee. She was cute, funny, a chain smoker and we got along great, so we made plans to see each other again for dinner and a movie.

I suggested a number of different restaurants, but Nadia responded that we should just hang out at my place, watch a movie and order some food. So I'm thinking 'Netflix and Chill'.

Anyway, those plans went sideways when Nadia casually mentioned that she was fasting for Ramadan. Since I'd met her in a nightclub and she'd mentioned alcohol, I hadn't realised she was Muslim and so I had no idea what I was supposed to do on our date.

Should I make a move? Is it culturally insensitive to make a move during Ramadan? Can I have a drink in front of her? I was totally confused and clueless.

I figured I should at least try 'something', so I reached over during the movie to take her hand. You know, some high school type stuff. This did not go over well. She basically froze for several seconds, before letting go of my hand and telling me she, "Didn't like holding hands." She then reached for her phone and sent a message while we continued to watch the movie in awkward silence.

About 10 minutes later she received a call and told me that her friend had broken down and she had to leave at once to pick her up. I simply shrugged, nodded and wished her well.

A month later I ran into Nadia (drunk) at a beach party. She introduced me to her boyfriend, who she had been dating for several months. I scrubbed all her contact details from my phone.

Eugene, UK, Designer

Forget About Dating Qatari Women

If you're arriving in Doha from a typical western background, your interaction with veiled women will almost certainly be limited. So finding yourself attracted to a Qatari woman in an abaya can come as a shock.

One minute you're being introduced around the new office, being mindful not to offer your hand to women unless they do so first, and then you meet her…

Now obviously this comes down to personal preference, but there's a certain type of Qatari woman with a darker skin tone, more angular features and Cleopatra-style eyes that's impossibly beautiful. And totally unavailable…

There are several reasons why it's never going to happen and they breakdown like this:

1.   Despite its modern façade, Qatari is still a deeply religious and traditional society. Arranged marriages are still the norm, and until recently marrying one's cousin wasn't considered weird or unhealthy. Basically, Qatari women are reserved for Qatari men.

2.   Due to the above, Qatari women don't date. They certainly don't date westerners. And they super especially don't date infidel westerners. Getting involved with a foreign man would cause a huge family scandal and seriously impact a women's marriage potential. Is your ass worth the hassle? The answer is almost certainly 'no'.

3.   Whoever the girl ends up with will almost certainly have more money than you, simply on the basis of them being Qatari.

4.   You're not Muslim. And therefore you're going to hell. Religion might not play a role in your life, but it's kind of a super heavy deal in Qatar.

5.   A million other reasons including the reaction of friends, society, the inability to go anywhere together and basically 'reasons'.

Despite all of the above, it's not unheard of for Qatari Women to secretly date westerners. And the key word here is 'secretly'.

This story can't possibly be true

One of the strangest stories I ever heard in Doha involved a drunk British expat, a woman in an abaya, a freshly cooked steak and two Saudi dudes.

According to the guy telling it, he was in an elevator leaving a house party when a woman in an abaya entered. They struck up a conversation and she invited him back to another apartment in the same tower. Not sure what to make of all this, but intrigued by this offer from an attractive woman, he accepted.

Upon entering the apartment he found two men in thobes already there watching television. Feeling distinctly uncomfortable, the expat went to make his excuses and leave, but the men insisted he should eat something and sent the woman to the kitchen to cook him a steak. After a little small talk the steak arrived, the expat ate it under everyone's watchful gaze, said his goodbyes and went to leave, escorted out by one of the men.

As he was heading down the hallway and towards the door he could hear the other man start to beat the woman he had met in the lift. He stopped to intervene but was assured it was none of this business and to walk away. Rather than follow this advice he turned around and stormed back into the living room. The details get a little hazy at this point but, according to the expat, he ended up leaving with the woman, took her to his car and drove her back to his house where they had sex.

Dan, UK, Oil guy

White Women Get All the Attention
(Whether They Want it or Not)

Dating is one of the few areas of Qatar life where the odds heavily favour western expat women.

As previously discussed, women are a minority in Qatari, comprising just 25% of the total population. But when you subtract all the local women, maids, and those who have already been promised to someone in an arranged marriage, the real figure is more like one single woman for every nine guys.

In other words, available women are a rare commodity in Qatar. That means they're automatically more attractive and more in-demand. So if you're a solid 7 back home, you'll instantly be an 8 or 9 out here. Congratulations, you're now officially 'hot'.

...And that means plenty of unwanted attention.

Getting hit-on and sexually harassed by guys is just a fact of life for western women. This comes from every direction and includes expats, foreign athletes, publically masturbating construction workers and local Qataris.

That last segment is especially persistent. Qataris are known to follow women home in their cars, approach them at the shops, on the street and anywhere else you can think of.

Attend any nightclub in Qatar and you'll find the place filled with local guys popping bottles at private tables and inviting women to join them. Technically, they're not supposed to be there (because sex and alcohol, etc.), but as long as they don't wear a thobe everyone turns a blind eye.

And here's where it gets ugly.

There is a perception in parts of the Muslim world that white women are mostly hookers and sluts — because obviously a bikini and a Tinder profile makes you a total whore.

That sort of thinking is a minefield that we're not going to get into here. Suffice to say, western women tend to have more liberal views regarding love, romance and dating than your typical local.

Qatar women are envious of this freedom, while local men may misinterpret it as something else entirely. So yeah, you might get plenty of attention, but most of it will be unwanted.

Still, there is a certain allure to living in a foreign country and dating a local. A romance with a rich and handsome Arab guy is a much better story than dating some British guy who works for a petroleum company. Unfortunately, 90% of the locals that approach you will do so because they think you're an easy lay they can keep on the side while they await their arranged marriage.

So, that leaves random expat bros and imported athletes who will cheat on you before heading home in six months time. Which means you're pretty much damned if you do, damned if you don't.

Dating a Qatari Guy

Qatari women are expected to remain virgins until their wedding night. Those same rules don't apply to the guys. In fact, they're free to sex as many hookers and/or western expats as they want.

As long as a Qatari man eventually marries a nice local girl and makes some babies he's given carte blanche to 'sow his wild oats' in the intervening years. Sure, he'll have to put up with some nagging from his mother, and some gentle 'tut tut' comments from the relatives, but for the most part he's free to do as he pleases.

That usually means a private booth at an upmarket nightclub, a large bottle of vodka, and inviting foreign women to join him and his buddies for shots while the latest 'club banger' plays in the background. To quote R.Kelly...

"After the show, it's the after party
And after the party, it's the hotel lobby
Yeah, around about four you gotta clear the lobby
Then take it to ya room and freak somebody"

All good and well, we're adults and we can make our own choices. But here's the thing; whatever kind of romantic relationship you may have with a Qatari man, it's almost certainly a placeholder. When push comes to shove, he's going to marry and settle down with a local girl.

This is the unwritten rule underpinning all relationships between Qatari men and western women, and it's why families and local authorities don't pay them any mind. You're simply 'the girl on the side'. This only becomes an issue when your presence threatens to derail an actual marriage. That's when all hell can break loose.

My girlfriend's gay boyfriend

My friend from the U.S. was living with her Qatari boyfriend for several months. This wasn't an issue until his family started shopping him around to local brides and he failed to express much enthusiasm for any of them. At this point the mother and sister of the guy showed up at the apartment, confronted his girlfriend and threatened to call the police on her for being a hooker. The couple broke up soon after... Oh, and the guy ended up being gay. But that's another story.

Hillary, U.S., Teacher

If a Qatari man is married and looking for a little action on the side, the polite thing to do is pay for his mistress' apartment and visit discretely in the evenings. Said mistress will usually be named Anastasia and come from Eastern Europe. A typical cover story would be something like "she's my English tutor." And while that all sounds like a pile of bad clichés layered on top of one another, it actually happens A LOT.

Thanks for the memories

Sarah was a very attractive 20-something architect from Spain. Her boss was a 40-year old Qatari who liked to hang out in clubs and 'party'. Within weeks of her arrival in the country they were an item. He paid for her apartment, bought her a convertible, etc. This lasted for two years, until one day he announced his engagement to a young Qatari woman. And that was the end of that…

Hookers in Doha

Officially, there are no prostitutes in Doha. Of course that doesn't tell the full story. Compared to Dubai (where you can't walk into a club without being knee deep in prostitutes), Doha is certainly a lot more discrete. The unwritten rule being you can do what you want (as a man), so long as you keep things quiet and don't attract any undue attention.

While Dubai offers an international selection of hookers (with varying rates for Russians, Africans and Asians), Doha tends to lean towards low-rent Filipinos. The Waterhole at the Sheraton used be the epicentre of the action (until it was razed in 2014). On any given weekend you'd find strung-out Filipino broads sitting on the laps of sweaty 50-something expat dudes. It was not a 'good scene'.

Whatever your opinions on sexing hookers, the ones that hang out in Filipino bars in Doha are unlikely to have you reaching for your wallet — unless of course you dream about strung-out, middle-aged Asian women wearing Phil Collins *Groovy Kind of Love* t-shirts.

Fancier hotels and bars also feature hookers, and it's not unusual to see Eastern European girls hanging out by themselves and just sort of swaying quietly by the bar while a line of guys approach them.

There's also the high-end escorts. Their whole shtick is they don't look like hookers, e.g. the airline stewardesses who will go on 'dates' in exchange for a new Prada bag. One such girl would ask her gentleman callers to wire her money for a new handbag if they wanted to 'hang out.' Curiously, her friends didn't really consider this prostitution because, new luxury handbag = not a hooker.

Of course prostitution is totally illegal in Qatar. But it's another one of those laws that tends to get overlooked unless someone is caught red handed and it makes the news, i.e. dead hooker in the hotel room drama.

A simple Google search for 'escorts in Doha' will bring up plenty of options. Prices for these ladies start at around 2000 QR for an hour (about USD $600), which isn't cheap, but this is a seller's market. Conversely, a random Filipino lady from a bar might be around 500 QR (USD $150).

Of course picking a hooker from an online profile and 'making a date' comes with plenty of associated risks. Aside from never knowing who's actually going to show up, it's also a really easy way to get shaken down and blackmailed by criminals or bored Qatari security forces.

Casually Sexy Times

In case you were wondering, condoms and personal lubricants are readily available in supermarkets. They're in the same products section you'd find in the west.

Things get complicated when it comes to actually having sex. The laws themselves are pretty clear-cut. No sex before marriage. No living together until you're married. Technically, these laws apply to both Qataris and expats. The difference is most westerners openly ignore them.

Go to any Doha nightclub and you'll see strangers leaving together at closing time. In that respect it's no different to any other western country. Keep it discrete and there's rarely a problem. Still, there are things to keep in mind...

A lot of expats live in company provided housing and share an apartment block with their co-workers. Normally this isn't an issue. But you probably don't want to run into a colleague at 2am with a Romanian hooker passed out in your arms.

Some companies also have curfews for employees; which means they may have to be back at a certain time, or they're not allowed guests after a certain time (usually 2am). Obviously this complicates the sexing a little.

In the more uptight residential towers it's standard policy to record the coming and going of all guests. Break curfew (or have an unauthorised guest over) and you may well have to explain yourself to your company's HR department. Qatar Airways are particularly vigilant of their female staff, and will happily dismiss someone on little more than rumours and innuendo.

Even if you live in an apartment that doesn't monitor guests, you can still upset the neighbours if you keep them up at night with sex noises. And yes, that is enough grounds for them to call the cops on you as some sort of sex deviant infidel.

There's also a double standard to consider when it comes to sexy times. While men having 'female friends' stay over is grudgingly accepted by even the most conservative of neighbours, any women who routinely brings home men is putting her job at risk. If the company finds out, they can dismiss her for any number of reasons. In other words, the guy's apartment will almost always end up being the preferred option for 'hook ups'.

Still, when it comes to getting laid, most western expats will happily ignore the official rules and take their chances. And this extends to hotels. While only married couples are supposed to share a hotel room, it's a law that Qatar uniformly ignores. Check into a four- or five-star hotel here and no one will ask you about your relationship with the other party... Try and check into a cheaper hotel and you don't deserve to have sex.

But We're Defacto

Any international job offer in Qatar will include either company housing or an accommodation allowance. If you're married you're entitled to a larger apartment or a bigger allowance. You also get various other perks and benefits for your spouse.

But the crucial word here is 'married'. Even if you've been together for 10 years and have a kid, the Qatari bureaucracy will not recognise it as an official partnership. Which is why you hear about couples having shotgun marriages before moving over here. Whether this has any affect on divorce rates is an anthropological study waiting to happen.

Trying to bring over a partner you're not officially married to is a logistical nightmare that we're not even going to try and explain here. The underlying principle is that every expat has to be 'sponsored' by someone — either an employer or their spouse.

If you have a 'partnership situation' that isn't legally recognised the easiest solution is a temporary tourist visa. Basically your partner comes over on an unrelated tourist visa and then ducks over to Dubai every few months to have this renewed. It's far from ideal, but it's easier than trying to explain your same-sex relationship or the concept of 'defacto' to a Qatari government official.

Couples who meet in Qatar don't have to worry about any of the above. You can simply move in together and ignore the law about un-wed couples living in sin. This is rarely a problem since western expats won't care, and the locals will be too polite to ask if you're legally married. But technically, it is against the law.

No homosexuals please; we're an arts organisation

An employee's homosexuality made the front page of the local papers when a Human Resource Manager for a well-known arts organisation granted a senior employee a 'spouse package' for him and his gay partner. The Qatari women handling the paperwork refused to process the request, so the western HR manager forced it through. Shortly thereafter the story was leaked to a prominent Qatari newspaper columnist, made the papers, and saw both the employee and the western HR Manager sent home.

Porn and Internet Filters

Qatar introduced an Internet filter at some point to block 'prohibited material'. But for our purposes, let's think of it as a porn filter, because that's the only time it should affect your browsing.

Like any other government filter, it's entirely useless and can be bypassed in a couple of minutes. Simply find yourself a reputable proxy server site (search for VPNs) and pay the subscription fee. You'll now be able to choose which 'country' the Internet thinks you're logging in from, i.e. the U.S., U.K., Europe, etc.

This not only bypasses the Qatari web filter, it means you can also subscribe to things like Netflix, Hulu, Spotify, etc.

Sex Shops and Adult Toys

While it's easy enough to access porn in Qatar, adult toys are another matter. As you can probably guess, there are no 'sex shops' in the country. In fact, there are no sex shops anywhere in the Gulf region. At least not officially, and the secret ones aren't advertising.

If you're looking for adult accessories your only options are to order them online or hide them in your luggage following an overseas trip. Neither method guarantees success.

As discussed elsewhere in this book, Qatar doesn't really have a postal service, so everything gets sent to a huge mail exchange where you send drivers to collect stuff. Aside from the very real possibility that your shipment will get lost, forgotten or stolen, you also have to contend with Qatar customs agents. These guys are surprisingly diligent and have no qualms opening and inspecting larger parcels. They will not be pleased to find a vibrator, dildo or weird sex junk being shipped to the country.

If you want to avoid customs agents (or significantly decrease their likelihood of seizing your butt plug), the best option is to use a freight service like Aramex or similar. The containers can still get searched, but they're far less likely to discover your weird sex kinks when they're packaged up in amongst a bunch of other stuff in boxes.

The final option is to simply purchase your sex toys overseas and ship them back on your flight. A few tips if you plan on going down this route:

1. Remove the product packaging before your flight. A bright box that says 'dildo' and features a naked

woman is hard to dispute. The more high end products on the market can be passed off as 'massage aids' if it comes down to it

2. Always place the sex toys in your checked luggage. A customs agent x-raying your bag won't notice anything suspicious. If someone starts poking around in your carry-on it's a lot harder to ignore a giant vibrating penis

3. If you get busted, feign ignorance, claim it was a joke gift for a friend's wedding (for instance) and go get yourself a strong drink.

Pregnancy in Qatar

If you need a reminder about where you are, just remember that Qatar considers 'unwed' pregnancy a crime. Technically, they can throw you in jail and then deport you for making a baby without a husband. In reality, this only applies to maids brought in from poor overseas countries (no one would dare throw a white woman in jail for being pregnant), but that doesn't really make it any better.

Jail time or not, most employers will immediately fire and deport an unmarried pregnant woman without giving it a second thought. It's also illegal to leave the name of the father off the birth certificate. Oh, and abortions are obviously illegal.

In other words, you don't want to find yourself pregnant and unwed in Qatar. Your options in that particular scenario are limited:

1.	Go overseas with your partner and have a shotgun wedding
2.	Go overseas and have an abortion

3.   Leave Qatar for good
4.   Get fired / deported — maybe thrown in jail.

What About the Homosexuals?

It should go without saying that homosexuality is deeply frowned upon in Qatar. Sodomy is against the law and can get a person between 1 and 3 years jail time.

But like most things in Qatar, the official policy and the reality don't necessarily line up. Anecdotal evidence suggests that there's actually a lot of girl-on girl and guy-on-guy action behind closed doors.

If you want to play armchair psychologist you can attribute this to a lack of interaction between the sexes, the tendency for women to be married off to their cousins, or broader cultural issues dating back centuries. But the reality is probably more straightforward — Qatar, like any other place on earth, has a gay and lesbian population.

Unlike neighbouring countries, Qatar has no interest in locking up or persecuting homosexuals. The authorities are much more comfortable pretending they don't exist and looking the other way. This can be challenging when an impossibly flamboyant Qatari pulls up to work in his hot pink Ferrari blasting Britney Spears and solicits the help (true story), but Qatar is pretty good at ignoring uncomfortable truths.

Spend a little time in the country and you'll encounter openly gay people from a variety of backgrounds. While we shouldn't generalise, it's hard to imagine the effeminate Filipino waiter who serenades dinners with Gloria Gaynor's 'I Will Survive' going home to a wife and kids. Likewise, the middle-aged Indian man in tight leggings and crop top at the club…

And then there are all the Qatari ladies who (supposedly) like ladies.

Point is, Qatar isn't the puritanical gay-free zone it paints itself as being. As long as you don't put yourself in a position where your homosexuality becomes an embarrassment for your employer, the police or the general public, no one really cares. In Qatar, homosexuality is treated the same way as worker exploitation, substance abuse and the Easter Bunny. It simply doesn't exist. At least that's the official line, and everyone is much happier accepting it at face value.

Let's hold hands, guy

Within days of my arrival I began to notice that South Asian men would often walk down the street holding hands. Since being gay is officially banned in Qatar, I thought this was a little odd. When I mentioned this to someone they pointed out that it's a cultural thing, and that two guys from India or Nepal holding hands means something quite different to their Sydney or Soho counterparts.

James, Australia, Marketing

Multiple Wives

Having multiple wives is considered 'chill' and 'fine' under the Qur'an. If you're particularly ambitious and stupid you can have up to four! Imagine! But that's a whole other article, and one we don't have room to entertain here.

All you really need to know is the practice still exists in Qatar, although having more than one wife is increasingly rare and usually associated with the older religious crowd. Like young families in the west, most newly married couples in Qatar are too busy trying to buy a house, get their life together, make a baby, etc, to worry about bringing another woman into the mix. That's what extramarital affairs are for…

Anyway, yes, polygamy is a thing in Qatar. But it's not really brought up in polite company — even though the former Emir has three wives, including the very prolific Sheikha Moza (his second wife and mother of the present Emir).

Where to Meet People

Tinder: Tinder is not a 'good scene' in Qatar. It's filled with women from the Philippines who describe themselves as "simple" and talk about God in their profiles. The men are no better, with a depressing run of misogynistic idiots from the Gulf and creepy Pakistanis who can't wait to send you an unsolicited cock photo.

InterNations: This is the easiest way to meet foreign randoms, but that doesn't say much about the calibre of people, or the shitty conversations at shitty restaurants you'll have to wade through to meet someone worth drinking with. But yeah, InterNations is basically a dating scene disguised as 'networking'.

'In da club': If you're desperate to make a connection there's always this fallback. One thing about Qatar is that pretty much everyone is a newbie and looking to make friends, so you can actually strike up conversations with people in clubs and build a posse that way.

Work: Expats will usually make an effort with the new arrivals and take them out to some house parties or bars. If you work for a large government organisation with a bunch of foreigners, it only takes one drunken party to meet people and go home with a solid '5' because "what happens in Doha stays in Doha."

At the Mall: Just kidding. Like, you can try it, but you're just going to look like a creep and get yourself deported for sexually harassing a local woman.

The Local Flight Crew

If you're looking to relive the drunken sex, binge-drinking, morning-after regrets and cheap gossip that characterised your college / high school years, you need to get in with the flight crews based in Doha. Collectively, they encapsulate every stereotype you've ever heard about the airline industry. In other words, they're a lot of fun.

Doha is home to both the Qatar Airways staff and the private crew that man the royal family's fleet of Boeings. While the Qatar Airways staff have curfews and schedules, the private flight crew are an entirely different beast. Gathered from the far corners of the world, they live their life on call — waiting for the text message that will tell them Sheikh so-and-so wants to fly to Tahiti (or wherever), and that they need to report for duty in 8 hours.

Until that message flashes on their phones, they're free to do whatever the hell they like. That might mean several days in Doha with nothing to do but get drunk and sleep around.

It's a surreal lifestyle and one that obviously isn't for everyone. What you end up with is a group of women (and men) in their mid to late 20s with lots of time and money on their hands. This creates a fairly tight-knit group of people who are always out together, getting drunk together and falling into bed together.

Essentially, it's a game of sexy musical chairs. But since everyone is always flying around the world, the group dynamic tends to switch up from week to week and sometimes people forget who it is they're supposed to be sleeping with.

That's when the fun starts — and the inevitable tears. Someone may come back from a two-week trip and discover that the person they were 'seeing' got drunk and slept with their best friend. Or, just some random from a club.

All of which makes for some great stories and fun nights out. But the overwrought drama is up there with a high school musical and can get real old, real quick.

As an aside, flight crew date THE WORST guys.

Type #1. Athletes with no personality. Since Qataris aren't real big on playing sport, the country tends to import all its athletes from overseas and give them temporary citizenship. That's a whole other issue. The point is, there's lots of 'dude bro' foreign athletes in town, and they all hang out in the clubs with their posse.

Airline stewardesses like these guys because they're obviously super fit and healthy. The fact they have no personality doesn't really matter because the next overseas flight is only ever a few days away.

Type #2. Rich Arab guys. Self explanatory; they have money, they own a boat, they have a private table and all the alcohol you can drink. You do not have these things, presumably.

Section 4. The Practical Stuff

---Shopping and Retail---

Local Shopping Malls

Hanging out in shopping malls is Qatar's favourite pastime. It's closely followed by bad driving, obesity and hypocrisy.

But at least the shopping makes sense. When you live in a giant construction site in the middle of a desert, ignoring the outside world for a spot of retail therapy and Star Bucks frappachino is probably the right choice.

Speaking of malls, here are the main ones and what you need to know about them.

City Centre (where dreams go to die)

Established in 2001, City Centre is one of the largest shopping malls in Doha. It's also old, rundown, lacking in retail options, and infused with a broken, back alley ambiance.

The first thing you'll notice about City Centre is that it's virtually impossible to find any parking. Ever. You could be there at 9am on a Tuesday morning and you'll have to wait at least 20 minutes while the line of LandCruisers in front of you slowly roll up to the toll booths.

Pro tip – you can save yourself a lot of time and heartache by parking across the street at The Gate Mall (which is way upmarket and always empty), or just valet park at the Marriot Renaissance (which is connected to the shopping centre).

Make your way inside, and you'll be struck by how dimly lit City Centre is. This is because half the light bulbs in the ceiling have blown out, and no one has bothered to replace them. Because, reasons…

If the lack of parking and poor lighting don't dissuade you, the limited retail options should do the trick. For some reason the mall is overrun with sporting goods stores. Something like 40% of the retail space is dedicated to health and fitness. This is deeply ironic in a country where physical activity is about as popular as pork.

The fashion options are just as disappointing. There are a number of smaller department stores selling overpriced designer labels, and a host of cut-price boutiques from Spain that you've never heard of — probably because no one from an English-speaking background would ever dream of shopping at a women's retailer named 'Jennyfer', but that's a whole other story.

If you really want to experience the sense of fail that hangs over City Centre then make your way towards the back of the mall where you'll find entire wings closed down and shops selling products that look like they were stolen from a Chinese pirate ship.

The icing on this expired cake is the discount store on the top floor. Featuring endless rows of cheap towels, t-shirts and electronics, the miserable selection of goods is complemented by sad people navigating consumer hell. Oh, and good luck finding a shop clerk to help you if you want to buy something behind the counter.

Villagio (death and luxury)

Villaggio is what happens when a rich Sheik visits Venice, decides he likes it, then finds the cheapest contractors available and asks them to build a rough approximation in the middle of the desert (see also Fake Venice #2 at The Pearl).

Opened in 2006, Villaggio is divided into two distinct sections: a regular shopping mall and a VIP wing dedicated to luxury brands.

The main bit features various western boutiques looped around a fake Venetian canal (complete with gondolas you can ride). The individual promenades have been 'inspired' by Italian city streets and the ceiling painted to resemble a Tuscan sky.

While this is an 'okay' idea in theory, the execution is half-assed. What was supposed to be a blue sky looks ominous and threatening, like the calm before a thunderstorm that puts a tree through your bedroom window.

Make your way past the food court (complete with ice skating rink), and you'll find the VIP wing. This section has its own valet parking and is where Qataris go to buy all their Louis Vuitton, Bulgari, Burberry etc, etc.

The thing about Villaggio is that A LOT OF PEOPLE DIED THERE. Back in 2012 a fire started in the middle of the mall and, Qatar being Qatar, 19 people (including 13 kids) failed to escape due to dubious safety measures. This is still a touchy subject and certain people were calling for the entire mall to be destroyed in the aftermath of the tragedy. Obviously this didn't happen, and to this day some people still boycott the centre because of it.

Land Mark (hard to find)

If you want a comfortable middle ground for your shopping then Land Mark is probably your best bet. It offers a good cross section of stores, plenty of parking, and you won't feel like killing yourself from dealing with the crowds.

The tricky part is accessing the place. If you're on the Doha expressway the off-ramp is several kilometres away and not clearly marked. So it's easy to overshoot and accidentally end up gunning it towards the Saudi border. Even if you know this from previous visits, you will, inevitably, miss the exit each and every time.

Lagoona Mall (sex and rumours)

Small and upmarket, Lagoona is situated across from the Grand Hyatt and features a selection of international boutiques. There are also various food outlets, a Carrefour and an official Apple reseller.

But the real action is centered around *Sugar n Spice*, the faux English coffee shop. Overflowing with young and fashionable Qataris, this place has a reputation for being a pick-up joint. Sort of like those bourgeois cocktail bars with the cougars back home — only here it's cakes and abayas. Which means it's an excellent spot to grab a coffee and watch the notes being passed and the awkward first dates.

Hyatt Plaza (sad and forgotten)

The redheaded stepchild of Qatar's shopping malls, Hyatt Plaza gets no love. Even though it's situated right next to Villaggio people ignore it like a homeless drunk screaming obscenities. Which isn't really fair given it has ample parking and a decent selection of food and retail options. But then the world isn't supposed to be fair.

Gate Mall

The main reason for visiting Gate Mall is to grab lunch at Jones the Grocer — an Australian café that does its best to recreate the inner-city aesthetic of Sydney or Melbourne. Beyond that you can do some window-shopping at Givenchy, Armani, etc., and play 'which shop assistant looks the most bored'.

The Mall

Not really a mall, just Mega Mart, a chemist, a coffee place, a bunch of western expats buying overpriced groceries and local scam artists circling the car park looking for suckers. But we'll get to that later in this chapter.

Shopping for Clothes

Shopping for clothes in Qatar sucks. While generic international brands like H&M and The Gap are present and accounted for, that's sort of like going to a restaurant and being told they're only serving cheeseburgers and Pepsi. You're not going to starve, but it's not particularly ambitious.

On the other end of the spectrum, Louis Vuitton, Buggati, Gucci, etc., all have their own retail shops here. The problem, obviously, is that unless you're a Qatari national you're not going to be able to afford them.

That leaves a whole lot of questionable brands you've never heard of before. Wonder around Villagio, City Centre or any of the other larger malls and you'll see retail chains like Jennyfur, Pull and Bear, Polo Sport Co and others doing their best impression of better-known, better-quality labels.

A quick Google search reveals that they originate from countries like Spain, Portugal, and several lesser European countries. While that's all fine and good, you wouldn't want to be caught wearing these clothes. No conversation worth having has ever included the phrase, "Yeah, I bought this at Jennyfur…"

To be clear, we're not here to judge your dress sense. This is Doha, wear whatever the hell you want as long as it doesn't get you arrested. The problem is there's no real alternative to this middle of the road 'blah'. The small independent boutiques you'll find in Europe, the U.S. and Asia simply don't exist out here. So if you want to buy something "way too exclusive" or are the type of person that follows fashion blogs you'll need to do your shopping while overseas.

---The Souqs---

Souq Waqif

When you first arrive in Doha, someone will inevitably take you to Souq Waqif, aka 'the standing market'. It's one of the city's main tourist attractions and dates back around a hundred years. Originally an old-school bazaar, it's been rebuilt and expanded over the last decade, accommodating commercial enterprises alongside the faux 19th century facades.

People love this place because it allows them to take 'authentic' Middle East photos within easy reach of a Baskin Robbins and Dunkin' Donuts. Meanwhile, the narrow laneways are filled with small shops selling tourist trinkets — if you're in the market for abayas, silk scarves or carved wooden camels this is the spot. Delve deeper and you'll find South Asian men selling a bewildering array of random household goods, but that's not very exciting, so we'll just keep this moving…

The main thoroughfare hosts a variety of sub-standard restaurants showcasing different culinary aspects of the Middle East. Expect a bunch of Lebanese, Turkish, Moroccan, Egyptian and Indian restaurants.

Although these restaurants help sell the idea that you're in some authentic market from the last century, the food tends to be fairly average. For the most part you'll find a selection of meat and rice dishes seasoned according to geographic origin. While there's nothing inherently wrong with these meals, the novelty tends to wear thin after a couple of visits and some 'just okay' experiences. Also, they don't serve alcohol, so you'll be drinking a selection of teas, coffees and tropical juices.

That being said, Qatar makes a mean juice drink. Seriously, they're really, really good. The usual selection consists of orange, kiwi, strawberry, mango and maybe watermelon. While the orange juice is exactly what the name suggests, the others have been infused with magical unicorn dust (or just a ton of sugar), and are a party waiting to happen in your mouth...

Still, there's no escaping the fact Souq Waqif feels like it's been designed for tourists. So if you want a more authentic experience you're going to have to dig a little deeper.

Falcon Souq

Located adjacent to Souq Waqif, the Falcon Market is about as Bedouin as Qatar gets. And yes, it's exactly what it sounds like. Whether you're looking to purchase a new bird, upgrade your old bird or just window-shopping, it's THE place to buy. Centered around a fully-functional, 24-hour falcon hospital (yes really), it's an entire city block comprised of falcon shops.

How 30 different shops selling the same variety of bird manage to stay open for business is a mystery, but it seems like the guys who run them like to just hang out and talk shit to each other. Which is nice.

Walk into one of these places and you'll usually find a few older Qataris guys sitting around sipping tea while a South Asian employee attends to the birds. Maybe owning a falcon shop is the Qatari equivalent of old men playing checkers in the park — a chance for bros to be bros?

Each of these shops house between 10 and 20 birds. You'll find them perched on stands in a large sand pit and mostly they just sit there quietly with their eyes covered by ornamental leather hats. Occasionally you'll see one gnawing away at a piece of meat on a bone.

Falcon prices vary wildly, and are determined by their size, pedigree and training. You can pick up an untrained, entry-level falcon for a around USD $1000 (3000 QR). For one of those-award winning, Rolls Royce falcons that the Sheiks own, you could blow USD $300,000 (1,000,000 QR) without breaking a sweat.

Tourists and visitors are welcome to wonder around the Falcon Souq and concoct weird fantasies about having a falcon sit on their shoulder during business meetings (in order to intimidate other people in attendance.)

And a plane ticket for my feathered friend

Falcons are so highly regarded in Qatar that they're required to fly Business Class when travelling with their owners. They're perched on a special stand and have their eyes covered during these flights. Amusingly, when the plane first takes off the flacons think they're being launched into the air and will start flapping their wings like maniacs before realising — wait! False alarm! They will then pretend like nothing happened and self-consciously peruse the latest issue of Forbes.

Gold Souq

The Gold Souq sounds a lot more exciting than the reality. While the name evokes an Arabian Nights style bazaar in Morocco, the reality is a dank old mall with a bunch of tiny little shops.

Granted, the shops sell some very elaborate jewellery and can create custom pieces for reasonable prices, but it's hard to get over the disappointment of the souq itself. If the whole place hasn't been razed to the ground by the time this book comes out it will be a minor miracle. Or just a damning indictment of Qatar's slow progress. Still, if you're under instructions to buy gold jewellery or looking for gifts, you'll find plenty of options here.

Used Furniture Souq

If you want to experience the squalor of a third-world market (without the associated flight), then head on down to the Furniture Souq. If nothing else, it will provide a stark contrast to your sheltered five-star hotel, valet parking, fine dining existence in Doha.

Located in Najma it's like a weekend car boot sale in a Pakistani slum. Taking up a full residential block, the market is comprised of narrow streets lined with tin-shed warehouses selling an ungodly mix of junk. Although furniture is the main focus, you'll also find merchants selling a bewildering mix of second-hand shoes, random electronics, blinds and who knows what else…

The souq is popular because in a country with spiralling inflation, and a huge population of poorly paid immigrant workers, it provides a budget alternative. All of which is great for the 1.5 million workers looking for a cheap wardrobe or cut-price bedding, but it can be an uncomfortable experience for western expats not used to slumming it.

For one thing, the furniture aesthetic is probably not going to appeal. Those of us raised on a lifetime of IKEA catalogues and Scandinavian minimalism may find the tassels, colours and faux decadence on offer confronting. The fact that all these design flourishes look like they come from the 80s doesn't help matters either.

The strange men who stalk you throughout the market can also unnerve the westerner shopper / sightseer. Because all of the items available in the market are sold on the spot and delivered on the same day, guys with trucks tend to follow anyone with a hint of money. This becomes somewhat farcical when several men form an impromptu conga line behind you as you make your way through the market.

If all of the above doesn't spell it out, then let's be clear, the furniture souq is not a place you want to spend your weekends. Its one saving grace is the fact they offer nondescript wardrobes at an affordable price. While only a crazy person would purchase a used couch here, the wardrobes are assembled on the spot, serve their function, and are about one-third of the price you'd pay at even the cheapest retail outlet. So there is that. But the rest of the products are an exercise in failure and shame.

Animal Souq

You can tell a lot about a country's animal welfare record by observing its stray cats. That might not be a hard and fast scientific rule, but it's one we're going to run with here.

Travel to Japan and you'll find some of the fattest, best maintained street cats in the world. Most of the ones you'll find in Tokyo wouldn't look out of place in a pet food commercial — all shiny coats and wide-eyed enthusiasm. Strays in Europe or the U.S. may be a little rougher around the edges, but you don't want to avert your eyes and cross the street when you see them.

Then there's Doha. If there were some sort of international award for pet abandonment Doha would almost certainly win. The streets are awash with stray cats and most of them appear on the precipice of death. Little more than bags of skin and bone, they look like any sort of physical contact would transfer a terrible skin disease.

Fact is the Middle East has a very different relationship with animals. Dogs, obviously, are a problem out here, in that they're viewed as 'unclean' animals. They're certainly not considered domestic pets that you would allow into your home (or take for walks). And while you'll see the occasional dog owner on the street it's still kind of awkward.

Cats are a different. Fancy looking pure breeds are common household pets, especially among younger Qatari women. The problem is the vast majority of these cats are not neutered, and if they give birth to a litter there's little in the way of animal shelters or support services. Which then loops back to where we started and all the abandoned, wretched-looking cats you'll find hanging out on street corners trying to sell you cat nip.

But seriously, it's a problem, and much of it stems back to the Animal Souq, which is where most of Qatar buys its pets. A hodgepodge of street vendors located in narrow laneways, the Animal Souq sells everything from cats and dogs to turtles, birds and God knows what else. Unfortunately, the conditions are appalling, with dehydrated, stressed and malnourished animals kept in small cages.

Maybe that's all part of the sales technique, because it's hard to look at these poor animals and not feel compelled to purchase one in order to save it. But since none of the cats have been fixed, wormed or otherwise prepared for life in the real world, a significant number die, get knocked up or otherwise find themselves living on the streets. Which is all a massive downer.

---Food and Groceries---

Your Favourite Fast Food Restaurants

You'll find all the usual fast food chains present and accounted for in Doha. From McDonalds and KFC through to Applebee's and TGI Fridays, they're scattered throughout shopping centres, strip malls and this one particular section of town that's known locally as 'Cholesterol Drive' in Al Sadd.

Fair warning — anything that should contain pork is going to taste 'weird' and 'wrong'. A pepperoni pizza is a case in point. Since pork is obviously banned, restaurants use beef or turkey substitutes. The problem is 'beef pepperoni' smells and tastes like food poisoning and failure.

Maybe if you've never had the real thing you wouldn't notice, but anyone arriving from the west can confirm there is a HUGE difference between real bacon and the beef or turkey kind.

Beyond that, you don't need a guidebook to tell you if you like McDonalds or Burger King, or whatever.

No Pork Please, We're Muslim

Gulf countries do not like you eating pork. You should already know this if you're planning on moving here. But just how much they dislike you eating pork varies from country to country. In Dubai they're pretty much 'whatever'. Qatar does not share this view.

Acquiring pork in Doha is sort of like buying booze, only more restricted. The only place you can purchase it is the one giant bottle shop that serves the whole country. In order to buy anything there you need a special license, which you have to have approved by your employer.

And while you can buy alcohol at five-star hotels in Doha, order a club sandwich and you'll be bitterly disappointed. Delicious, real bacon will have been replaced by either beef or turkey bacon, both of which completely defeat the purpose.

You can read more about the Qatar Distribution Centre (QDC), Qatar's only pork sales outlet elsewhere in this chapter.

Grocery Shopping

As mentioned above, you won't find any pork products in Doha supermarkets. No salami, no ham, no bacon or chorizo, etc. This is your new, pork-free reality.

But it's not all bad; the grocery stores out here carry a reassuringly familiar range of products. Your favourite breakfast cereals, confectionary and whatnot should all be present and accounted for. You'll also find various regional quirks, i.e. entire spice sections, Filipino breakfast cereals and Saudi brands that try their best to disguise this with names like 'Americana'.

Still, not all supermarkets are created equal, and the price and selection you'll find in Doha's supermarkets varies a lot more than it would back in the west.

Carrefour

The most established retailer in Qatar, Carrefour is reliable, but rarely amazing. If it were a musician it would be the *American Idol* finalist whose name you can't remember. Or something sort of like that…

Oh, and just like every new season of *American Idol*, standards have been on the slide. Popular international brands have been disappearing from shelves, replaced by 'Carrefour' imitations. While these are cheaper, no one moves to the Middle East to purchase discounted, home-brand products.

Fresh

This is where you'll find Filipinos and faux-hippy westerners. The Filipino crowd shop here because the stores tend to be located in working-class neighbourhoods and the prices are reasonable. The hippies because they're assholes who think they can realign their karma by pretending they're poor.

Either way, the fruit on display looks old and 'nasty'. So unless you need to pop down the local shop for some bread/milk/butter, these are probably best avoided.

Mega Mart

If you're feeling homesick and craving that one particular brand of biscuits or cereal that you used to purchase in the west, this is the spot. Mega Mart specialises in imported goods from the U.S. and U.K. (and isn't shy about charging you for the privilege). To make this even more dubious, they'll have identical items stocked next to each other, with drastically different prices depending on whether the label is in Arabic or English. *Pro tip: The products all come from the same place and taste identical.*

Mega Mart earns extra kudos for the scam artists who circle the parking lot preying on unsuspecting westerns. What happens is a LandCruiser with some Arab guy and a veiled woman will pull up alongside you as you're heading to the car with your shopping. He'll explain that they're from Saudi, and need petrol money to get back home across the border.*

Faced with this unusual request, the newly arrived westerner will panic and hand over whatever money is on hand. After all, the guy has his whole family in the car and when has an Arab ever lied about anything? Another variation involves an elderly man in the passenger seat who requires urgent medical care.

Whatever the story, it's a scam. These people spend their day circling the car park preying on westerners who assume that anyone in a thobe or abaya is deeply religious and would never resort to cheap scams. Because Allah, obviously…

Still, you can have fun with these people. One approach is to listen to the story with a concerned look on your face, get out your wallet or purse, and saying something like, "Well I've only got (USD $150) 500 QR, would that help?" At this point you'll see their eyes light up and all sorts of blessings come tumbling out of the guy's mouth.

This is your queue to reach for the money, act like you're about to hand it over, pause for dramatic affect, then say, "But 500 QR isn't that much. I'm sure the local police will be able to assist you. Let me call them now and see if they can organise more money for you."

The driver will start to back peddle at this point, tell you that your kindness is more than enough, and that please-could-he-just-have-the-money-now, thank you goodbye. Ignore all this, get out your phone and start making a big production about calling the police to come assist him in his time of need…

Then watch the car speed off into the distance, and notice that it doesn't have a license plate.

*A full tank of petrol costs nothing in Qatar.

Spinneys
Spinneys is supposed to be the more upmarket shopping option for expats, but really, it just looks like a normal supermarket anywhere else in the world.

Monoprix
Upmarket French supermarket that has electronic prices on the shelves for all their goods (convenient) and a little café that will make you fish and chips (nice touch). Good luck finding a parking space.

Local Convenience Stores

Say what you will about convenience store franchises like 7-11, but at least you have a rough idea of what to expect. For whatever reason, these chains never bothered setting up shop in Qatar, and so the market is dominated by a hodgepodge of local independents.

These neighbourhood bodegas offer an unpredictable mix of products, customer service, food hygiene and expiration dates. Always check the expiration dates!

But the real fun is trying to actually pay for your purchases. During busy periods you'll find a selection of South Asian men yelling over each other and throwing money at the hapless clerk while demanding an assortment of cigarettes and phone cards. Your natural instinct will be to hang back in an orderly fashion — this is wrong and useless. Unless the clerk takes pity on you, you'll be standing in your imaginary line for days.

The only way to successfully complete a purchase is to push your way to the front (don't be afraid to use your elbows) and place your goods directly in front of the clerk. Subconscious memories of western colonialism will compel him to serve a white person first.

If that all sounds like more trouble than it's worth, you can avoid the rabble and call up your local convenience store to request a home delivery. Or just double-park outside the shop and honk your horn like an asshole until some kid comes running out to take your order. Qatar is lazy like that, but that doesn't mean you're allowed to just give up on life and join in. So maybe think about that before dialling the store and requesting a packet of cigarettes and some Red Bulls.

No Qatari Food, Thanks

There are no Qatari restaurants in the Souq, or anywhere else, because no likes Qatari food. This includes the locals who were raised on it.

For the most part, it's a mish-mash of Arabic and Indian influences. At large gatherings it's usually spiced rice with a whole cooked lamb on top. That's all fine and good. The problem is Qatari food is never actually cooked by locals. Rather, it'll be some poorly paid Filipino maid or Indian peasant doing their best impression of Arabic food while someone yells at them to hurry up. This is not conducive to great culinary feats.

Occasionally a Qatari work colleague will bring a selection of local treats to the office to celebrate an occasion. In this instance the food will be a sugary and gelatinous selection of sweets with way too much cumin and probably a pot of lima beans on the side. Nine times out of ten it will have been prepared by their maid, who just wants them out the door so she can watch her Indonesian soap operas and have a little peace and quiet.

The polite thing to do in these instances is the same as it would be in any other country — take a small sample, proclaim it delicious, then return to your desk where you can set the food aside to throw away later.

But back to the original point; You won't find any Qatari restaurants because the locals aren't interested in cooking it, and the 'fusion' stuff that's whipped out of the 'help' is as bland and lifeless as the desert landscape.

---Media and Entertainment---

Magazines, Newsagents and Bookshops

While it would be cruel and incorrect to refer to Qatar as a cultural wasteland, it's not a country that places much value in books, literature or media freedoms. If that sort of thing is relevant to your interests you'd do well to invest in a tablet and a VPN account to hide your online location before boarding the flight over.

Newsagents simply don't exist out here and finding English language publications is an exercise in futility. If you get desperate you can hit up the Virgin Megastore or larger supermarkets, which stock basics like *Esquire*, *Monocle*, *Time*, *Newsweek* and a handful of women's gossip magazines.

The bookshops are equally sparse and 'sad sams' when it comes to their range. Qatar is one of the few countries in the world where the introduction of a WH Smith had people queuing outside at the official opening. As it turned out, the local branch mostly consisted of Dan Brown novels and airport pulp.

If your reading range extends beyond this, then you're out of luck. There's no Penguin Classics to speak of in these WH Smiths and if you happen to ask the staff about, say, Ernest Hemingway, they may well reply, "Is that the name of the book or the author?" That said, they do a fine line in *Dora the Explorer* backpacks and pencil cases…

A number of other, older bookshops also exist in Doha, the most notable being Jeremiah Books, which also doubles as an electronics and stationery shop. This should tell you all you need to know about their selection. Suffice to say, you're not going to find any Bret Easton Ellis novels on their shelves.

In short, you're going to be downloading a lot of books for your tablet if you want anything that isn't going to turn your brain to moosh.

The Local Papers

Qatar has two main English language papers: *The Peninsula* and *Gulf Times*. While neither publication is going to win a Pulitzer, they provide a decent enough snapshot of local and international news. They're also very fond of featuring the Emir on the front page. Seriously, it's a rare morning where the Emir isn't on the front page BEING AWESOME and shaking some guy's hand.

While there's no 'official' censorship of the papers, it's hardly necessary. All the editors know exactly what they can get away with (very little), and do a fine job self-censoring their content appropriately. Criticising the government or the royal family is obviously out, and since they also own all the country's main industries, you're not going to see much criticism of anything. Basically, the newspapers are a place for feel-good PR stories.

If you want a first hand example of just how blasé the papers are about journalistic integrity simply forward them a press release. As long as it's accompanied by a decent photo, you should see your hyperbolic nonsense appear word-for-word in the next available edition. Which obviously makes for pretty depressing reading. Although it's kinda great if you work in PR and need stories planted to keep your boss happy.

The thing is journalism isn't really respected as a career out here. And no one in Qatar will read a book if they can help it. So words on paper don't really carry the same meaning they might for, say, the readership of *The New York Times*. At the end of the day, the papers in Qatar are an opportunity to sell ads and keep the advertisers happy with nice stories about their latest entry in the *Guinness Book of Records*. That's it.

Doha News Dot Co

If you want any real news on what's going on in Qatar you're going to have to look at digital options. Dohanews.co publishes the sort of investigative stories that no one else out here will touch. Or at least it did. The site was geo-blocked in 2017 due to a 'lack of official license'. It's still active, but you'll need a VPN to access it within Qatar. Aside from that, your best bet is Twitter.

Social Media

Qatar is one of the most connected countries in the Middle East and everyone who isn't a dinosaur is on Facebook, Instagram and Twitter. Especially Twitter. In fact, most Qataris carry two mobiles with them at all times, an iPhone and a Blackberry — the latter used almost exclusively for BBM (Black Berry Messenger).

While the rest of the world had pretty much retired Blackberries by 2011, their continued existence out here comes down to one simple reason — their encryption means authorities can't monitor them*. Whether that sort of paranoia is warranted is beside the point, BBM is deeply ingrained in social life out here. As late as 2013, you'd still here stories about Qatari guys scouring the malls for local girls to shout their BBM number at.

Questionable pick-up attempts aside, we don't have room to get into the dos and don'ts of social media here. Presumably, most people reading this already know the basics, i.e. don't post anything you wouldn't feel comfortable sharing with a room full of strangers, private accounts aren't actually private and can be accessed easily enough, only a fool openly criticises their employer on Facebook, etc.

Social media in Qatar throws a number of extra caveats into the mix. But all you really need to remember is that criticism of the country, the ruling family, or Islam is a sure fire way to get yourself jailed and/or deported. There is no such thing as free speech out here and there are specific laws against levelling any sort of public criticism at another person.

Actually, the idea of 'constructive criticism' really isn't a thing in the Gulf. And since even your private social media can be screen-grabbed and forwarded on to anyone who might be interested, you'll find yourself self-censoring your posts much more than you would in the west.

Because of all this, people's social media feeds can take on a demented, Ren & Stimpy-esq vibe of 'Happy Happy Joy Joy'. While friends back home are posting photos of their cats, drunken boozing or whatever, Qatar feeds soon turn into a sociopathic mix of fancy hotels, imposing skylines, swimming pools and local quirks.

Inevitably, your friends back home will assume that your new life is an orgy of decadence and excess. What they don't see is all the day-to-day drudgery and bullshit you have to put up with out here. And the fact you can't post about any of it on a public forum.

Another local oddity is that while Qatari women all have their social media accounts, almost none of them will post pictures of themselves. Qatar is super weird about protecting its women from outside hoards. One of the ways this plays out is an 'unofficial' ban on photos being posted in the public sphere.

If you do add a Qatari woman on social media (because, for instance, you want to show people outside work how hot she is), you'll be bitterly disappointed. In most cases her entire photo album will be nothing more than photos of her pet cat. Which at least is in keeping with the broader theme of the Internet.

*May not actually be true

Censorship

As you can probably guess, censorship is a big thing out here. Despite its claims to being a modern, forward-thinking country, Qatar loves to censor stuff. Especially anything that could be construed as halfway sexy, i.e. sexy pictures, sexy movies, sexy South American labels on chilli sauce (true story).

While the country's complete ban on porn shouldn't come as a surprise, it certainly doesn't stop there.

Movies are a case in point. Hollywood blockbusters are reworked to ensure anything approaching sex hits the cutting room floor. While you can sit through two hours of people killing each other in gruesome ways, you will never see a married couple kiss, because obviously the cinema would descend into heavy Sodom and Gomorrah vibes.

While this doesn't have much impact on the annual *The Fast and the Furious* sequel, it means anything approaching a mature, adult film, is a complete waste of time at the local cinema. Which is why everyone just gets a VPN and watches illegal streams at home.

Fun Fact #1: Qatar censors cut a full 45 minutes (or one-third of the running time) from *The Wolf of Wall Street*. The movie that eventually made it to cinema screens was a surrealist in-joke with plot holes you could fly a Qatar Airways Dreamliner through.

Fun Fact #2: Leonardo DiCaprio and Carey Mulligan never actually kiss in the Qatar version of *The Great Gatsby*.

Magazines are another example of Qatar's ridiculous censorship rules. The first time you open an imported title and find that an image of a woman has been blanked out with marker you'll probably stare at it for several minutes, take a photo, and forward it to your friends back home with an accompanying 'WTF' comment.

Then the grim realisation dawns on you — somewhere in Qatar there is a warehouse filled with foreign workers whose sole task is to manually go through magazines and obscure the offending images of women who dare show a little shoulder. Or an ankle. Or whatever.

Hot girls for my hot sauce

Okay, so the movie and magazine censorship can (maybe) be attributed to heat madness. But nothing can explain the Hula girl illustrations that were blanked out on bottles of hot sauce in a local supermarket. Presumably, the combination of hot sauce and buxom women on the label was considered too much for local sensibilities. Although any link between hot source and rape is yet to be established by a reputable scientific journal.

Offending Mah Morals

What's most troubling about censorship in Qatar isn't the act itself, but the justification behind it. Officially, these images are deemed morally offensive and blah, blah, blah. But the unspoken message is that men are unable to control themselves and that the sight of a woman's shoulder or a couple kissing on screen can turn them into unwitting sex offenders. Which is insulting to both men and women.

Unfortunately, this is country where victim-blaming still prevails. The sort of place where people would rather tell women to cover up than tackle men's attitudes towards sexual harassment.

Granted, Qatar isn't as bad as Saudi Arabia, but that's like saying [insert your favourite dictator) wasn't as bad as Hitler.

The IKEA catalog is another weird manifestation of this censorship. In the Saudi Arabian version someone photoshopped out all the women in the family images – leaving just the men and their sons. In order to avoid the outcry that accompanied the Saudi edits, Qatar simply avoided using any images of people in their catalogue. Either way, the underlying message is the same.

---Getting Around Doha---

Qatar isn't a big place. You can drive from the northern tip to the Saudi border in the south in about two hours. Doha is even smaller and comprises a few key areas. But the horrendous traffic that gridlocks the city can make it feel much more substantial. Everyone drives everywhere and there's no real public transport to speak of.

Since the city is such a nightmare to navigate, knowing where to live and how it will impact your daily commute, is kind of important.

West Bay

West Bay is the fancy part of town you'll see in all those skyline shots of Doha. It's where all the hotels, office towers and residential apartments are located, and where the rent is the most expensive. If you're planning on going out in Doha nine times out of ten you'll find yourself hanging out somewhere around here.

Because of its close proximity to everything, West Bay is the preferred haunt for western expats. That also means rental prices are astronomical and, unless you're a director or CEO, you'll probably find yourself sharing an apartment with two or three other expats.

The trade-off is you usually have a nice gym and pool area in the apartment complex, and you can stagger home drunkenly from nights out at The W, The Sheraton, Four Seasons, etc.

Oh, and the traffic is notoriously rubbish. Since West Bay is the epicentre of commerce in the country, getting around during peak hour actually means sitting in your car and not moving.

Al Sadd

Al Sadd is one of the Doha's older districts and is currently being redeveloped. How many years this will take is anyone's guess, but all the old 60s and 70s buildings are being razed and you'll find entire blocks that look like the setting for a post-apocalyptic space movie.

The area used to house a bunch of foreign labourers but they've all been kicked out and sent to the industrial zone. In their place you'll find middle class expat families from North Africa, Asia and the wider Middle East. They're all housed in beige tower blocks that will be lucky to stand ten years given the extremely shoddy construction work by Indian labourers who give exactly zero fucks.

Al Sadd is also home to what is known as 'Cholesterol Road', a wide, grid-locked boulevard featuring every second-rate fast food establishment you could ever hope to avoid. From Arby's to Burger King and Dairy Queen, this is where you go to pack on the kilos.

Or, if you prefer dodgy Lebanese dudes and Romanian hookers, La Cigale hotel is located along the same drag and is home to both a rooftop cocktail lounge and the super skeezy Piano Bar (try it on Sunday nights after midnight for the full horror show).

Musherieb

Musherieb is where you live if you're poor. Not South Asian labourer poor, but like, Egyptian family of five on one-income poor. It's an old district with a bunch of crumbling buildings from the 1970s, nightmare parking scenarios and mangy looking cats hanging out on street corners. Usually, it smells terrible.

By the time this book is released that may have changed, as the area is undergoing massive redevelopment works. According to artist renders they want to create a modern residential and commercial hub with an underground subway network linking the area to the rest of Doha.

It all looks really nice and impressive on paper, if perhaps a little too wholesome and centrally planned. But Doha being Doha, the timeline is in a constant state of flux, and no one really knows when any of this will be finished and inhabitable.

In the meantime, the whole area is a dark and dank construction site — not somewhere you'd actually consider living or want to hang out in.

The Pearl

This is Qatar's answer to Dubai's man-made residential island (The Palm). It's a huge USD $20 billion construction that is supposed to house something like 45,000 people when it's completed — that may be some time, because the whole complex has been plagued by issues from the get go.

Originally pitched as a high-end development full of exclusive retailers and major international restaurants, the reality is a ghost town with row after row of shuttered businesses.

Things went south when the development ran into financial difficulties during the GFC and the government had to step in. One of the conditions for state funding was a ban on alcohol sales (one of the major selling points of the original restaurant-lined boulevards). That decision saw a bunch of internationally recognised eating establishments close down and visitor numbers hit single digits.

Since then management has tried to rework The Pearl as a more inclusive development with cinemas, supermarkets and mid-range burger joints alongside the residential towers. All of which is fine, but it doesn't really justify the outrageous rental prices or the inconvenience of only one entry/exit from the island — which means huge traffic jams when someone inevitably rolls their LandCruiser on a flat stretch of road for no apparent reason.

The Pearl is also home to a fake-Venice development known as Qanat Quartier. While the canals are all there and accounted for, and the buildings are painted lovely pastel colours, it's mostly a ghost town with empty shops. Still, there's a public beach and if you drink enough booze and squint you can pretend you're in Venice.

Industrial Area

This is where dreams go to die. Literally. All those poor souls from South Asia that were lured to Qatar with the promise of fair salaries and dignity were rounded up back in 2011 and forced to live out here. This is so their filth and poor morale wouldn't negatively impact the rest of the population.

As the name suggests, the Industrial Area is a hellish mix of light and heavy industry, wretched supermarkets, graveyards for old trucks, car service centres and depressing housing complexes where several guys from India share a single room.

In a bid to address criticism that the government was segregating the labour population, the industrial area has been provided with a new sports complex and shopping precinct in recent years. But some people would argue this simply reinforces the notion workers should stick to their little dirt patch and not sully our eyes with their presence.

For obvious reasons, the western expat population goes out of their way to avoid the Industrial Zone. This works fine until you need to get your car serviced. When that faithful day arrives you'll get hopelessly lost navigating the poorly signed overpasses and service roads, get stuck in traffic, witness the poverty firsthand and learn what privilege really means.

Alternatively, you can farm the task out to a local fixer and enjoy another Manhattan at your favorite hotel lounge.

---Buying a Car in Qatar---

The Basics

If you live in Doha you're going to have to buy a car, no two ways about it. As previously mentioned, there is no public transport to speak of, cab drivers are notoriously dodgy, you can't walk anywhere, and it's not practical to 'call your driver' or request an Uber every time you realise you're out of toilet paper.

Admittedly, there are some people who steadfastly refuse to play along and will lean on friends to give them lifts. This is unacceptable and shows a selfish disregard for 'the way things work'. It can be particularly troublesome in the morning when you're forced to carpool someone from work and feel compelled to maintain a 'conversation' even while you're dying on the inside from the previous night's binge drinking.

So yeah, buying a car. First up, if you have a British or Australian passport you can simply go into the transport department and have a local driver's license issued on the spot. Trying to do this without any Arab language skills is an exercise in fortitude, so the best thing to do is find a local 'fixer' and have them deal with the paperwork and the ladies at the department on your behalf.

Thankfully, there are plenty of friendly Arab men loitering outside the transport centre who will happily assist you — for a small fee. Save yourself a lot of trouble and pay them. Oh, and don't worry about finding them, they'll see you, the confused westerner, coming a mile away…

If you're from the U.S. or elsewhere then you'll have to actually take lessons and pass a driving test before they'll give you a local license. From all accounts this is a hellish process that will take years off your life. If you already know how to drive your best bet is to try and find a local fixer who can 'deal with it' and get your international license converted to a local one.

Or you can just risk driving on your international license. Technically you can drive around Qatar on one of these for three months. It's not going to help you much if you get into a car accident (which happens, like, A LOT in Qatar), but, if you're stopped by police for one of their roadside checks, you should be able to continue on with minimal fuss. Not that we'd recommend this approach...

Also, if you're from a country where people drive on the left hand side, or just follow the road rules in general, it's probably best to adjust to Doha's roads with a rental car. Compared to most places, renting a car in Doha is dirt cheap, a basic compact will set you back around USD $500 (2000 QR) for the month, and that includes insurance. You can then crash your underpowered Chevy Sonic (or whatever) as many times as you like and simply leave it by the side of the road while you go get another one.

Actually Buying a Car

It's important to realise that you can't outdo the Qataris when it comes to cars. They all make more money than you. The best you can really do is go for something mid-range and respectable. Obviously this is a matter of personal opinion, but you're not going to get any respect on the road pushing a Nissan Tiida or a Sunny.

The thing about the Qatar car market is that luxury cars tend to drop in value pretty quickly after a few years. That means a BMW, Audi or Mercedes with a couple of years on it can look like a bargain. Which it is — until it develops crippling mechanical faults that cost a fortune to fix.

Look under my bonnet

Car dealerships in Qatar have a complete monopoly on whatever manufacturer they represent. The lack of viable alternatives means these service centres can charge whatever they want for parts and service. They exploit this ruthlessly.

If you purchase a luxury car out of warranty you better hope it's in good condition. Simply driving your car into a service centre and having someone look under the bonnet can easily run you USD $500 (2000 QR).

They also have a tendency to give you apocalyptic, worst-case scenarios on the state of your car. In one instance, an oil leak in a five-year old BMW 3 Series was diagnosed as a need to replace all the engine tubes, and estimated as a USD $4000 job (12,000 QR). When asked to identify the exact source of the leak, the consultant backtracked and grudgingly admitted they could probably just seal up the problem for USD $500 (2000 QR).

In other words, you should approach all repair quotes with deep suspicion. If you feel like they're trying to bleed you dry it's because they are. This is particularly galling when it comes to 'labour costs'. While the mark-up on parts is significant, these guys make their real money with ludicrously inflated service charges.

How they justify several hundred dollars in labour costs when everyone knows the mechanics are imported from South Asia and paid a couple of bucks an hour is one of those GCC mysterious which is too horrible to contemplate.

Dealerships and Private Sellers

There are used car dealerships scattered throughout Doha, but they tend to be small, hole in the wall places, where some guy has simply parked a bunch of LandCruisers on the footpath and retreated to an adjacent office where he can chain smoke in air-conditioned comfort. This blasé approach to selling cars can be somewhat unnerving for westerners, and you have good reason to be suspicious.

A better way to track down used cars is via websites like QatarSale.com, which allow private sellers to post their cars and offer a huge selection of models and price ranges. That said, buying a second hand car is always a gamble, especially when you're in the Middle East, super especially if you don't speak the local language.

A couple things to keep in mind:

1. If you buy a vehicle that's older than five years you're required to get an annual inspection in order to keep it on the road. More importantly, the desert air has a tendency to seriously damage cars not built to withstand it.
2. The Middle East loves to import cheap used cars from the U.S. and the market is flooded with GMC and Chevy 4WDs. The problem is these cars have absolutely no resale value and are known for chronic problems. Japanese and Korean cars tend to be better

built and will retain their value a lot more. The luxury European cars are somewhere in the middle.

Regardless of where or how you find a car, make sure you get it checked out before handing over any cash. There are a number of specialist car centres on Salwa Road whose sole purpose is to check cars for defects and potential death traps. They'll be able to tell you if a vehicle has been in an accident, has its original parts and is roadworthy. For added peace of mind, you can also check with the dealership that sold the car to see if it has a service history.

A cautionary tale

Dealing with local mechanics and having them certify a car is a slow and tedious process, but the alternative can be far worse. One optimistic expat found a BMX X5 with a few years on it selling for USD $13,000 (55,000 QR) — a lot cheaper than the usual price. He bought the car without an inspection and everything was fine… for the first month.

When he took the car to a mechanic because of strange thumping noises under the bonnet he discovered that the previous owner had rebuilt the car following an accident and filled it with random car parts from old Skodas. Getting it back into a driveable, roadworthy state was quoted at USD $10,000 (30,000 QR).

The LandCruisers

For lots of boring reasons (i.e. conformity, reliability, general on-road presence), most Qataris drive a LandCruiser. Or several. These 4WDs are totally inescapable in Doha and can make driving on the roads feel like something out of a Mad Max film, since local Qataris simply Do-Not-Give-A-Fuck about road rules.

Seriously though, LandCruisers — and associated vehicles such as the Nissan Patrol or Lexus 4WD — are a menace. Drivers treat the roads like it's still 1998 and barrelling through a round about at full speed while smoking a shisha and not looking is acceptable behaviour.

Other awesomely shit driving habits you can look forward to include:

- Tailgating drivers and flashing their lights at the vehicle in front to showcase 'ownership' of the lane
- Riding the shoulder to avoid traffic jams
- Mounting curbs and driving across footpaths
- Swerving across several lanes of traffic without indicating
- Muscling into non-existent spaces
- Showcasing displeasure at a fellow driver's actions by cutting them off and then hitting the breaks.

The basic rule of thumb while driving in Doha is to expect death and carnage at any given moment in time. Between the Qataris who believe they 'own' the roads (and have the giant SUVS to prove it), the terrified expats and the south Asians with a death wish and a Bangladeshi license, it's basically Hiroshima out on the streets.

---Other Transport Options---

Public Transport

Buses

Public transport is virtually non-existent in Doha. Yes, there is a bus service, but it's the least practical way to get around. It's also (unofficially) reserved for low-wage labourers.

Point is; no one moves to the Middle East so they can stand around a bus shelter in 40-degree heat and catch a ride with some South Asian labourers. If you're going to be stuck in traffic hell — which happens a lot — then you want to be as comfortable as possible. That means purchasing a luxury German SUV or as close as you can afford.

Taxis

Taxis in Doha are a slightly more viable option, but only in the short term. If you can actually find an available cab during peak times you can expect a variety of strange and unappealing odours emitting from within.

While cab fares are pretty reasonable compared to most anywhere else in the western world, the drivers have a tendency to claim their meters are broken and demand a set fee. They do this because they are charged a daily rate to use the cars and have to make a certain amount just to break even.

Knowing this doesn't make it any more comfortable for a passenger who's being quoted double the regular price by a shady driver. It's especially prevalent around five-star hotels late at night, where your only option is to haggle the price or stand around on a street corner waiting for the rapture... or dawn. Whichever comes first.

Private Drivers

A few years back having a private driver was one of the most convenient ways of getting around town. You could call 'your guy' 24/7 and know that he'd drag himself out of bed and drive you anywhere in town for about USD $10 (40 QR).

If you'd arrived from a country where simply stepping into a cab would cost you several dollars, this private driver shtick seemed remarkably cheap. It also means you didn't have to risk drunk driving, because 'your guy' was never more than a text message away.

Since then Uber has come along and commercialised the idea of a private driver to an international audience. So all the guys who used to work privately (basically hotel drivers moonlighting) have signed on with the phone app service.

In other words, if you don't have a car (or like to get drunk in hotel bars), it's probably a good idea to sign up for Uber in Qatar.

Gypsy Cabs

While Uber has corned the market for private drivers, vestiges of old Qatar remain in the 'gypsy cabs'. These are the guys that will honk their horn at westerners walking down the street and offer them a lift.

For the most part they're dudes on their way to work looking to make an extra buck. And since they never state a price, they rely on guilt-tripping you into coughing up cash with a, "Whatever you think is fair, sir."

It's basically the same as those lentil restaurants where you pay whatever you want — and inevitably pay too much.

Stepping into a stranger's car in the western world is a sure fire way of getting yourself hacked to pieces, but offering lifts in Qatar seems to be more about hospitality (and earning a buck) than any homicidal tendencies.

That said, women should be extremely wary of anyone offering them a lift. And stepping into a stranger's car in the Middle East probably isn't the smartest move for a guy, either.

Local authorities agree — the practice was officially banned in 2013 — but that doesn't mean you won't get honked at by some guy in a beat up Nissan sedan asking if you need a lift. Simply wave him away and live the rest of your life without getting hacked to death.

---Health and Fitness---

Watch Your Weight

If you're looking to let yourself go, the Gulf is an excellent place to add bulk. Six months out here can turn once svelte and athletic westerners into red-faced dynamos who struggle with a flight of stairs. There's even a local term for it: Doha Belly. It's caused by a perfect storm of sedentary lifestyle, high-fat diets, shitty weather and local customs. So let's look at that.

Four easy ways to add 'bulk'

1. Sitting on your ass
Qatar society is based around minimal movement. Whether it's driving to work, sitting at your desk or relaxing at home afterwards, people out here tend to spend their days in various states of reclining. Back home this might be interspersed with a quick walk to the train station or local café, or whatever, just to reassure yourself that you were in possession of functional legs.

Doha looks very unfavourably upon walking. Even if you arrive with the best of intentions, you'll quickly discover that getting around on foot simply isn't a viable option out here. Town planning (ha!) and infrastructure is based around giant, standalone complexes interspersed with a nightmarish mix of road works, dust, kamikaze drivers, searing heat and roadside bins that smell like decomposing bodies.

Fact is, there are no real 'neighbourhoods' to speak of. No local cafes, or bookshops or whatever. Instead, it's just random buildings that you're forced to drive between if you want to get anything done.

And there's the rub. While you probably took walking for granted back home, Doha really makes you appreciate how nice a short stroll is — simply because you can't do it. When you do find yourself travelling overseas you'll insist on walking totally impractical distances simply because it's such a novelty.

2. High-Fat Diets

All that sitting on your ass wouldn't be such an issue if you had a balanced and healthy diet. But that's not likely out here. Sure, you can cook your own dinner at home and prepare a nutritious lunch for work, but it's much easier to pick up something from the office cafeteria and then pick up something on the way home. Throw in all the random office treats, birthday cakes and drunken 3am meals at Dairy Queen, and you're well on your way to weight gain.

Also! Everyone delivers. Which means you can order a bucket of KFC directly to your door without having to ever leave the couch. You can then sit wallowing in your own crapulence with a drumstick in your hand.

3. Shitty Weather

As you're maybe aware, Qatar is hellish throughout the summer months, with the temperature rising as high as 50 degrees celcius (in the shade). And while you'll eventually grow to accept this, only a masochist would actually walk around outside voluntarily.

Granted it's quite lovely in winter, but that's only three months out of twelve. The other nine months will mostly be spent hanging around apartments, hotels, shopping malls and restaurants. None of which burn a whole lot of calories.

4. Big-Boned locals
Carrying around excess bulk is socially acceptable in Qatari and is still perceived as a mark of success and wealth. That said, it shouldn't be an open invitation to start shovelling food down your throat like you're competing in a Coney Island hot dog challenge. Besides, you're not wearing an abaya or thobe to disguise those extra kilos (at least you better not be).

And that's the tricky part. Out here it's real easy to lose perspective. That applies to a whole array of stuff, including weight. Because if you're surrounded by larger people, your own weight gain can seem relatively insignificant.
But when you consider that the Gulf has some of the highest obesity rates in the world and huge problems with diabetes, it's kind of like being the skinniest person at a fat farm — not exactly cause for celebration.

Remember, you have to go back home one day, and ideally you want to return richer, wiser and in better shape than when you left.

How to avoid getting fat in two easy steps:

1. Skip desert and watch what you eat
2. Join a gym, actually attend it at least a couple of times a week.

Finding Clothes that Fit

All the morbid obesity in Qatar means sizing is all over the place. Clothing labels don't like to make their customers feel like fat losers, so they rework the sizing on the labels to keep people feeling good. Small becomes extra small, medium becomes small, large becomes medium, etc., etc. This isn't confined to the Gulf; the U.S. has being doing this for years.

The difference is the U.S. has plenty of retail options. Qatar doesn't. And because shops are geared towards a local audience you'll find that even 'medium' sizing will envelope your frame. So while you were a perfectly reasonable medium back home, out here your business shirts are suddenly slim fit small. The same goes for dresses.

This is especially prevalent amongst strange, local retailers you've never heard of before, i.e. Jennyfur. The only way to get around this is to stick with western brands and their associated price hikes. Or just do like the other expats and purchase your clothes while overseas.

Gyms and Health Clubs

Qatar may not be big on the whole health and fitness thing, but that doesn't mean they don't have gyms. If you live in a modern apartment, you'll probably have a reasonably equipped gym located somewhere within the building. If you're lucky there might also be a pool on the rooftop. Larger office towers also have gyms and the like, so there's really no reason to let yourself go.

If you prefer a more regimented sporting routine there are also gyms in larger shopping malls. You can even join a boot camp group and go running around MIA Park with a bunch of other expats while some guy in cargo shorts yells at you to keep your knees up. Alternatively, The Corniche is a popular running spot during the cooler months.

There's also the Aspire Zone, aka Doha Sports City, which is a 250-hectare sporting complex located next to Villagio shopping centre. It features indoor running tracks, basketball courts and the whole nine, plus there are plenty of local teams you can sign up for.

If you want something a little fancier, the Ritz Carlton has a health club that looks like something out of *Wall Street* (the original one with Charlie Sheen). It's all polished wooden walls, private barbers, squash courts and hefty annual fees. But you'll also gain access to the hotel pool and can sit out by the deck chairs ordering drinks once you're done exercising. Most of the luxury hotels have a similar deal.

But honestly, all this talk of gyms and exercise is pretty boring, so we'll wrap it up here. The 'takeaway' is you'll find pretty much all the same athletic options as you would back home. Just don't try and exercise outside beyond the winter months, you will literally die.

---Staying Alive---

Medical Insurance

Any legitimate job offer in Qatar should come with health insurance. If it's a government position, you can expect a very generous annual cap that covers everything short of breast augmentation or a new head of hair.

Things aren't so clear-cut in the private sector, especially if you're a 'contractor'. Technically, Qatar has universal healthcare for all citizens and residents, but you need to be officially registered and have a local healthcare card to access it.

When negotiating your salary package ensure you ask about health insurance and cover. You can assume an organisation's attitude towards your physical wellbeing will translate to all other aspects of your employment. If they're trying to jerk you around on the insurance front you can be sure they'll do the same regarding pay, accommodation and everything else.

Without getting bogged down in boring details, that's pretty much it as far as medical insurance goes. So instead, let's hear a short story about Qatar dentists...

Qatar has a bunch of dentists from all over the world. The calibre of their service varies wildly, but if you're from a comfortable western background you'll want to use your available private medical insurance to go somewhere nice.

Help! They've taken my teeth

I was preparing to leave the country, so I figured it was as good a time as any to FINALLY have my crumbling teeth fixed and use up my medical insurance. I booked a session at an upmarket clinic and was attended to by a burly Egyptian guy who took some x-rays, noted I had three fillings that need fixing and booked me in for the procedure.

Now I get pretty nervous about dentists, and really hate the drill, so I appreciate all the painkillers and such that they can provide. Usually, that means a needle to numb whatever area they're working on.

I don't know where this guy got his training, but he was on some military shit. I didn't see or feel any needles, but he completed three fillings in under an hour without any pain. I mean, my mouth felt like it had been raped when I waked out of there, but the actual procedure itself was as quick and painless as anything I'd experienced in the west.

Adam, Canada, Construction consultant

STD Tests

While pre-marital sex is illegal in Qatar, it's one of those laws where unless you're caught red-handed with a government minister's daughter, everyone pretty much looks the other way. Which is maybe just a convoluted way to say there are medical clinics all over town that provide STD tests off the books.

If you want to keep things quiet and forgo your medical insurance, the tests are about USD $500 a pop (1500 QR). The staff are pretty blasé about the whole thing and since they're all from the Philippines or India, you're not going to get a lecture or be talked to about Allah.

That being said, Qatar seems to have a very laidback approach to condoms. Perhaps it's because AIDs is no longer considered a death sentence, or maybe it's because nothing feels real in the Gulf, but safe sex seems to be the exception, rather than the norm.

You can read more about all that in chapter on love and dating.

Smoking Cigarettes

If you're reckless enough to still smoke in whatever year this is, then you'll appreciate Qatar's (and the Middle East's) blasé attitude towards passive smoking. Firstly, cigarettes are dirt-cheap — a 20 pack of Marlboro Lights will run you about USD $3. Even better, you can smoke them practically anywhere.

With the exception of workplaces and government buildings, you're pretty much free to light up and enjoy 'flavour country' like it's still the 1950s. Hotel bars and nightclubs all allow smoking and if you're dinning at the one of the five-star hotels you can enjoy a cigarette at the end of your meal.

While it's almost inevitable that the region will tighten smoking laws in the years to come, it's still a free-for-all at the moment, so you may as well take advantage of it while you can. Hell, even if you've quit, you may want to consider taking it up again for a year or so — just because.

---Everything Else---

Importing Goods

True Story, I originally planned to import all my furniture and magazines and stuff from Australia to Qatar. I figured it would be cheaper than buying everything from scratch and the furniture allowance provided by my employer would cover it. I quickly gave up on that idea when I was told it would take five months for all my stuff to arrive (and I'd be living in an empty apartment in the meantime).

All of which is blah, blah, blah — the point, I think, is that when I inquired about shipping things to Qatar I was notified by the shipping company that customs agents here would trawl through the whole lot to make sure I wasn't trying to import porn, sex toys, drugs or anything else fun.

While I doubt they'd actually go through every single DVD case and box of magazines, I also didn't want them stumbling across a stash of weed I had forgotten about and hid in one of those DVD cases. Or some old *Playboy* I had written an article for and was keeping as reference.

And there's the rub, Qatar has the manpower and the boredom to search whatever you try and ship into the country. Which is something to keep in mind before you place an order for 'smart drugs' from the U.S. or a sex toy.

The 'Mail Service'

Following on from the above, Qatar doesn't actually have a postal service. Look closely and you'll notice that none of the houses or apartments have letter boxes. None. Zero. Zilch. Nada...

Turns out, this is a throwback to when Qatar consisted of several dozen families and some dhow boats. Back in the day there was one central post office to deal with all the mail and people would simply show up to collect their various bills and whatnot. Since the population of the country was so small it was a perfectly workable system and no one was in a huge hurry to receive shopping catalogues from Carrefour.

By the time the population started exploding in the early 2000s, introducing a postal service seemed archaic and wasn't helped by the general lack of street numbers. Instead, everyone scrambled to find a workable alternative, which ended up being a sort of ad-hoc delivery service to hotels and larger buildings.

Basically, if you want to avoid the nightmare that is country's only post office, you can have mail delivered to your work address or your hotel. As long as you work for a reasonable sized company you'll have staff dedicated to collecting and delivering the mail. Same for the hotels. Ask someone who's been in the country longer than you and they should be able to give you a rundown of what works and who to speak to.

That said, you'll still have to deal with extremely sloppy delivery times. It's not unusual to wait several weeks for an international delivery. Exactly why it takes so long is a mystery. Presumably it has something to do with an overworked postal system and a fairly blasé attitude to leaving your mail gathering dust for weeks on end.

If you don't feel like leaving your mail at the mercy of a clapped out postal service there are a number of alternatives. DHL offers express postage to anywhere in the world. The problem is the insane prices. Sending a regular envelope back home will cost you around USD $20. Anything larger than that and you're looking at giving up a full day's salary.

The other problem with international mail is that Qatar is often 'blacklisted'. Because of all the stuff mentioned above, companies like Amazon tend to list Qatar alongside Nigeria as a far as scams, 'lost mail' and fraud are concerned.

Thankfully, you can get around this with a global shipping services like Aramex. Simply register with the Qatari branch and you can have items delivered to the local warehouse for pick up. It's not going to help you with your day-to-day mail, but it's a godsend for overseas shopping.

Dumb World Records

Qatar is home to some of the most pointless world records ever attempted. This is probably related to the previous section and the points discussed — you can make up your own mind.

National achievements officially recognised by the *Guinness Book of World Records* include:

- Largest soccer ball
- Longest thank-you letter to a ruler
- Largest Monopoly game
- Biggest squash racket
- Largest t-shirt
- Largest shopping trolley.

Brunch in the Gulf

The first time I was invited to brunch in Qatar I went in expecting a typically western scenario. You know; coffee, eggs, an hour or so to catch up and be on your way. I was absolutely not prepared for what followed.

Brunch in the Gulf means something very different to its homegrown counterpart. Indeed, it's more like a four-hour binge drinking session with a buffet to help justify the debauchery. It works out like this.

Brunch starts around 12pm and lasts until 4pm. There's a fixed price to cover the food buffet and drinks. This will vary from venue to venue, but you're always going to be in a five star hotel so think USD $150 (500 QR) or thereabouts.

Also, you can forget about an intimate gathering of friends. Brunch in the Gulf means an extended entourage of friends, associates and hangers-on sat at a long group table.

But all you really need to know is these brunches are a chance to get ridiculously drunk in the middle of the day. And it's not like you have much say in the matter - the staff move from table to table topping up any champagne glasses that aren't full to the brim. So while you might go in with the best of intentions, it's very easy to loose track of your alcohol intake.

"Did I have four glasses of champagne or fifteen?" By the time things are winding down it's impossible to answer that questions. And since no one is in any state to drive, the party tends to relocate to an adjacent poolside location where someone will usually insist on shots. Soon thereafter it all becomes a blur and the last thing you remember is jumping into a stranger's car to crash a house party in a villa.

In other words, it's a serious commitment. Whereas brunch in the west may take two hours to reach a satisfying conclusion, in the Gulf you're looking at around 10 hours. So best to leave the car at home, take an Uber, and cancel any plans for the next morning.

Still, if you're new in town, a brunch invitation is a great way to meet people and expand your social circle.

(None boozy) things to do

The jaded expat will tell you there's nothing to do in Qatar but get drunk and spend money in fancy restaurants. This is mostly true. But it's not the whole story. There are plenty of wholesome, affordable things to do in the country. Here's a selection.

Picnic at MIA Park

The parklands surrounding the museum are great for picnics, offer a variety of small kiosks selling coffees and snacks, and even let you take small paddleboats out on the water. In the winter months they host a market bazaar. Whether you're looking for a family activity or just a little peace and quiet the parklands are great – except in summer, when they become a hellish 40-degree oven roasting in the desert sun.

Explore Katara Arts Centre

Katara Arts Centre is criminally under utilised. Located alongside the harbour it offers a variety of restaurants, galleries, shops and a theatre. But the real highlight is the wide boulevard that runs adjacent to the harbour... now if only someone would install some lighting and permit vendors to set up shop this would be a real destination.

Go dune bashing

If you spend any considerable length of time in Qatar you'll eventually find yourself in the back of a Landcruiser while a crazy Arab launches the vehicle over sand dunes and drives it at 45-degrees that make your stomach lurch. It's a miracle more people don't die.

Check out a camel race

They used to get small foreign children to ride the camels until someone pointed out that maybe it wasn't a good look. The children were eventually replaced by monkeys, but that wasn't really much better, so in the end the locals gave up and just let the camels race without any jockeys – monkey or otherwise.

November to February is peak season, and there's a virtual 'camel city' surrounding the Al-Shahaniya racing track, which is about an hours drive south of Doha. Alternatively, there's a dedicated TV channel for the races.

Wonder the Corniche

We're starting to grasp at straws here, but the Corniche does offer some lovely views of the harbour and a pleasant walk on a cool winters day. It's not going to change your life, but if you're looking for a place to go jogging or an excuse to get out of the house you could do worse.

Visit Mathaf: Arab Museum of Modern Art

If you're looking to impress one of those 'I like art type girls' Mathaf is a good place to start. A café and gardens mean you can grab a coffee or lunch after checking out their latest exhibition.

Take a road trip to Al Khor

The 'other' city in Qatar, Al Khor is a coastal town about 50kms north of Doha. So if you're looking for a road trip this is about as good as it gets.

Go Bowling

Okay, we're officially getting desperate for things to do now… But for the sake of thoroughness it's probably worth mentioning the bowling alleys.

Go ice-skating

If ten-pin bowling isn't your thing, a number of local malls feature indoor ice skating rinks. You can pretend you're in an American rom-com starring Tom Hanks and Meg Ryan or join one of the local ice-skating teams with all the other expat Canadians.

Catch a plane home

And when all else fails you can always drive to the airport, leave your car in lot, buy a one-way ticket home, and write a book about your adventures.

Understanding Ramadan
(and other public holidays)

In Qatar, like other Muslim country's, the main show in town is Ramadan. It's a month of dawn til dusk fasting to commemorate the first revelation of the Quran to Muhammad. It falls on the ninth month of the lunar calendar, so it's exact date will vary from year to year.

As a western expat you'll be expected to show respect and keep any daytime snacking private. That means wolfing down energy bars in office stairwells or toilet cubicles.

The good news is it means reduced office hours (generally 9am-2pm), long public holidays, and very little in the way of work or productivity. The end of Ramadan is marked by Eid-al-Fitr, which will see you get a week off work. This is followed soon thereafter by Eid-al-Adha, which should get you another week off work.

As a western expat all the above can be strange and confusing, but all you really need to know is that the country shuts down during Ramadan, and most people book overseas holidays to destinations where they can eat and drink during daylight hours.

If you do hang around expect all the hotels bars, bottle shops, and restaurants to be closed. Instead, everyone will stock up on booze and have lots of really drunken house parties.

Oh, and if you want to make a joke to your western expat buddies just suggest that the Qatar Public Service goes on holidays for Eid and doesn't come back to work until February in the new year.

Other public holidays

There are no public holidays for Christmas and Easter in Qatar. These are Christian (infidel) celebrations and as such they're not recognised. Sure, you'll see the shops get in on the action with displays and holiday products, but you're not getting an official public holiday or anything like that.

Sports Day – Feb 14. Falls on the same date as Valentine's Day, which is suspicious.

March Equinox bank holiday - varies

June Solstice bank holiday - varies

September equinox bank holiday - varies

December Solstice - varies

National Day – December 18. Marks the country's unification in 1878. Everyone drives up and down the Corniche in their Landcruisers honking their horns and blocking all the roads. If you have to be anywhere you're better of walking – the traffic *literally* doesn't move.

New Years Eve and New Years Day – Dec 31 and Jan 1. Because why not?

Imported Athletes

Like any country, Qatar loves to win awards and see its flag hoisted at sporting events. Unfortunately, the relatively small population, desert climate, and culture means that Qatar is not a country naturally predisposed to Olympic glory.

They get around this by bringing in 'riggers' from foreign nations, giving them a large bag of money and a temporary Qatari passport. It's a slightly unorthodox approach, but it means the country can claim gold medals in events it has no previous history in.

Which is what happened in 2000 when Qatar bought an entire weightlifting team from Bulgaria. Angel Popov, competing under the name Said Saif Asaad, claimed bronze for Qatar at the Sydney Olympics.

Or there's Kenyan born Stephen Cherono, who became known as Saif Saaeed Shaheen when he accepted Qatari citizenship and a chance to compete under the country's banner. He currently holds the world record for 3000 metre steeplechase, although panicked Qatari officials had to rush out and stop him making the Christian 'sign of the cross' when he won his first race at the World Championships in Athletics.

On a more local level, you'll find the football clubs, handball teams, and other sporting associations are mostly comprised of international athletes. These are the guys who weren't quite good enough to go pro back home, but can earn a lucrative salary and play sports for a living in Qatar. And it's hard to begrudge them that.

---Crime and Punishment---

Roadside Checks

Spend a couple of months in Doha and there's a good chance you'll find yourself caught in a roadside security check by the police. Think of it like a drunk-driving check in the west, except the police are looking for absconded maids and illegal workers.

The usual deal is they'll close off a main road and have all the drivers present their national ID. Don't worry too much about this as a western expat, they have minimal interest in you and, unless you're sloppy drunk, they'll wave you through, weather you have ID or not.

That said, you really should avoid drunk driving in Doha. The country has a zero tolerance policy and anything higher than 0% can get you fined, locked up and deported. Also, if you're involved in any sort of accident, you're automatically assigned fault if there's any trace of alcohol in your system — whether it was your fault or not.

Secret Police

Like any other country, Qatar has various strata of police, assigned to cover different areas. Listing them here is neither interesting, nor useful.

The ones you really need to worry about are the guys who look after internal security. While their main priority is to keep the royal family safe, they also maintain broader law and order in the country, and that extends to the supply of drugs and other vice.

According to various 'unofficial' sources, you'll find plain-clothes police in various bars and clubs keeping an eye on people. Qatar is small place with very tight-knit community. So you can pretty much assume that anyone who is operating outside the boundaries will attract attention.

How the security forces respond to any given situation will depend on a person's nationality, family connections and a host of other factors. But if your new found friends are popping bottles in the VIP and doing coke at the after-party there's a good chance someone in power is looking the other way. Or, maybe they're right there in the bathroom with you.

The Legal System

First things first, you don't want to find yourself at the mercy of the Qatari legal system. It's slow and archaic, has little regard for justice and assumes all foreigners are guilty until proven otherwise.

So if you ever find yourself in a situation where you may have to argue your case in a local court there's a lot to be said for simply driving your car to the airport, buying a one-way ticket home, and cutting your loses.

Seriously though, there's a long and shonky history of judicial 'prejudice' to wade through. Just Google French footballer Zahir Belounis or Al Jazeera Children's Channel (JCC) Manager Mahmoud Bouneb to read the horror stories. In both instances the men found themselves stuck in the country, unable to work, and at the mercy of a slow and indifferent legal system because of a falling out with their employer.

Or there's the case of French businessman Jean-Pierre Marongiu. He was trapped in the country after a dispute with his business partner and claims he passed bad cheques. The guy eventually lost his mind and kayaked to neighbouring Bahrain, where he was subsequently picked up by local authorities and deported back to Qatar.

But here's the real kicker; where a court action is filed against a Qatari the rules are reversed. Following the fire at Villagio shopping centre in 2012, it was revealed that the nursing centre where 13 children lost their life was illegally built. Also, it was owned by a Qatari diplomat, Sheikh Ali Bin Jassim Al Thani.

The accompanying court action stretched out for years, as the defendant repeatedly failed to show, and the judge simply adjourned to a later date.
Eventually, four years later, no criminal convictions were recorded against anyone involved.

Trapped in Qatar

No one thinks they're going to get barred from leaving the country… until it actually happens. A Canadian museum staffer I worked with was turned back at customs while attempting to fly out on an official work trip.

Turned out her employer had blocked her (and several other people) from leaving the country while they conducted an internal audit of all the pieces in the museum collection.

No one had bothered to tell her, or the other staff, and the Canadian embassy was unable to do anything to lift the travel ban. The woman had to wait several weeks before she was eventually cleared to leave. At which point she obviously resigned and left the country for good.

Civil Uprising

As has been noted earlier in this book, the ratio of Qataris to foreign workers is something like 30:70. In other words, Qataris are a minority in their own country. This can make them apprehensive, and the royal family goes out of its way to alleviate this with very generous social and economic perks.

Still, it doesn't take a genius to do the maths. If all those disgruntled foreigners were to rise up they could seize power through sheer numbers. And who would stop them?

As it turns out, that not-very-secret U.S. military base in the centre of the country has a duel purpose. According to (completely unverified) conversations with locals, the U.S. military is under orders to maintain the monarchy at all costs, and in the event of large scale civil uprising are authorised to roll into the streets and do whatever is necessary to keep 1.6 million South Asian labourers from claiming the country as their own.

Admittedly, it's far fetched scenario. But stranger things have happened. If nothing else the above should give you some insight into the unique tensions that exist in Qatar.

Section 5. Returning Home

---You Know it's Time to Leave When---

Depression in the Desert

"Every job package in Doha should include a free therapist… and Prozac."

The daily papers like to wheel out dubious surveys proclaiming 90% 'life satisfaction' rates among the local expat population. Feel free to mock and ignore these. They're usually little more than figments of someone's imagination or sourced from a very elite pool.

The reality is life in Qatar can be tough, and most westerners struggle with bouts of homesickness and depression at various times during their stay. Sure, there's perks, but living in a giant construction site manned by indentured labourers is not good for one's psyche. It's an emotional roller coaster and the longer you stay the more prevalent the mood swings become.

Granted, the first year isn't too bad — everything is so new and you're so busy drinking your way through house parties and hotels bars it's easy to numb your brain. Make it past the first 12 months and you're probably looking at a 3-4 year stint out here. That's when the reality starts to sink in.

Despite all the money, the luxury, the drinking and the general debauchery behind closed doors, this is a country where happiness is in dangerously short supply. And that goes for all strata of society.

The local Qataris have seen a huge influx of money over the past two decades, but at the same time they've seen their once quiet homeland transformed into a series of shopping malls and hotels where they're now a minority. This is especially bittersweet for Qatari women who are well aware of the freedoms available in the west, but can't walk into a licensed venue in their own country.

The plight of the construction workers should go without saying. The fact that no one ever bothers to include them in these quality of life surveys tells you everything you need to know about their daily existence.

And then there's 'white people problems'. Doha is a never-ending series of minor frustrations, and while they might not be huge on their own, they have a way of exponentially multiplying and wearing people down. The enthusiasm that you had upon your arrival will eventually be replaced by teeth grinding and calendar watching.

By the time you reach the two-year point you will have seen everything, met everyone, and realised that you're living in a frontier town where you have to drive 40 minutes into the desert to purchase alcohol from the lone bottle shop.
The annual trips back home will only serve to remind you what you gave up.

Common Complaints

Work imposed restrictions
The typical government department or satellite office doesn't much care what you do, as long as it doesn't appear on the front page of the daily papers. The service industry is a lot more 'protective' of its staff.

Qatar Airways is a case in point. Its flight attendants have curfews, aren't allowed to have guests after 10pm and are required to be in their apartments 10 hours before a flight.

Generally speaking, adults do not appreciate having their employers telling them what time they have to be back home, who they can invite back with them and if they're allowed to drink.

Relationship issues
As discussed in the love and dating section, trying to find and maintain a relationship in Qatar is grim. Five minutes on Tinder will confirm this. It's depressing just thinking about it, so we're going to move on.

Conservative society
While you can get away with a lot behind closed doors, there's no escaping the fact this is a very conservative society. Something as simple as a beer with your picnic can lead to arrest and deportation, which is a massive downer. The longer you stay here the more it gets to you.

A sense of powerlessness
Within a few months of your arrival you'll realise that your ass belongs to your sponsor (i.e. the company or organisation that brought you over).

At the risk of sounding melodramatic, the country can feel like a very well catered prison. Even your job contract, and the ability to resign and take another position rest on the whims of your sponsor.

And God help you if you get into legal trouble. Or in any kind of financial dispute with a Qatari. The guilty-until-proven-innocent nature of the criminal justice system out here means people have found themselves blacklisted from travel, fired from their jobs, unable to apply for other work and at the mercy of a court system that is as slow as it is biased against foreigners.

Day-to-day issues
Let's see, traffic is a constant nightmare, it's hot, that lactose-free milk you like may suddenly vanish from store shelves, you can't walk down the street because there are no sidewalks and even if there were there's nowhere to go, and yada, yada, yada. After a while you start to look around and wonder if it's all worth it.

The spiralling costs of living
Qatar has some of the most expensive rental prices in the world (on par with London and New York), and they keep rising. Annual salary increases simply do not exist for foreign workers and you can assume that whatever you start on is what you will end on. After a few years you'll crunch the numbers and realise you'd actually be better off back in London, New York, or wherever you call home.

Bureaucratic nightmares

Any dealings with a government organisation will require an infinite number of forms to be completed, signed, stamped in duplicate and delivered to several different departments. These departments will (almost without fail) lose the documents, requiring you to start again. The only way around this is to hire a local 'fixer'.

Should I Drink More and Care Less, or Just Up and Leave?

Faced with all the above, you have two options. You can either hit the bottle even harder and become a full-blown alcoholic, or you can back away from the edge and take stock of your life.

Doha is full of English expats who went with the first option. They're the ones drinking themselves into oblivion at the weekend brunches. These unfortunate souls have found themselves in a strange purgatory where they endlessly bitch and moan about Qatar, but they're so accustomed to the pay packets and perks they can't imagine ever going back to rainy, lowly paid Britain. So all that's left to do is open the next bottle of wine...

Alternatively, you can cut back on the drinking, stay sober for a weekend and suddenly realise you're not happy here when your brain isn't swimming in booze. This can be both liberating and deeply disturbing, because the moment you realise you're no longer having fun in Qatar you're basically doomed. It's like taking the Red Pill in the Matrix; you can't go back to blissful ignorance afterwards.

For most people this won't occur until they're seeing out their second year. But obviously it varies, and while some people get out after only a few months, others hang about for several years.

How to Actually Leave

If you're working in Qatar unofficially, i.e. your doing a 'visa run' to Dubai every couple of months, there's not much to it. You jump on a plane and you head home. In most cases your employer will pay for the flights.

Things get a lot more complicated when you're employed by a government organisation and your personal finances — such as your car loan and apartment — are tied to that same organisation.

On the surface, the rules are pretty clear-cut. You're supposed to provide two months notice and clear up any outstanding debts. If you do that you're supposed to be issued with an exit permit and (usually) a ticket home by your sponsor.

Like many things in Qatar, the official process and the reality are quite different. Indeed, a significant percentage of the expat population drives to the airport, jumps on a flight home and only notifies their employer that they're not returning when they're safely home and outside Qatar jurisdiction.

That's not some weird coincidence. Leaving Qatar can be incredibly stressful and convoluted if you try and do it via official channels. To assist with this, former expats have created a (unofficial) guide to getting out in one piece. Below are some of the highlights.

1. If you have an annual flight home courtesy of your employer make sure you claim it before you resign. That way you get both your annual flight home AND your end-of-contract flight back.

2. If your organisation offers annual bonuses they're unlikely to pay them out if you've resigned.

3. When you first start a job you'll probably be on three months probation. Any subsequent bonuses and perks are usually calculated from when you finish your probation, rather than your start date. Keep that in mind when planning your resignation and exit dates.

4. In many government organisations you won't get paid your salary during your notice period. You'll be paid this money in your final settlement (which takes into account any outstanding debts you may have, e.g. car or furniture loan). While timeframes vary, don't expect to see any money until about two months after you catch a flight home.

5. In most cases you won't be granted any more exit permits during your notice period. In other words, you'll be stuck in Qatar for about two months.

6. It's recommended that you pay off your credit card and close the associated account at least 45 days before your departure (otherwise your bank may freeze your funds to ensure any outstanding transactions are covered).

7. On that note, you should move as much of your money as you can into an offshore account. Qatar banks have been known to freeze accounts for fired or departing expats and it can take months of calls and emails to sort things out.

8. Your final settlement will be paid into whatever Qatar bank account you've been using to receive your salary. You can ask your employer to transfer it to your international bank account, but they'll most likely ignore those instructions.

9. If own a car you'll need to provide your HR department with a letter from the bank saying any loan amount has been repaid. Also, selling a car requires several kinds of forms to be processed. That's beyond the scope of this book, but a 'fixer' at the Traffic Department can help you with the insurance and transfer documents.

When All Else Fails

(Catch the Next Flight Home)

I'd heard all the stories. About the expats who drove their luxury cars to Dubai airport, abandoned them in the car park and bought a one-way ticket home during the Global Financial Crisis.

I'd seen it firsthand too. Staff members who went on annual leave and emailed to say they weren't coming back.

So when it came time to leave Qatar for good I wanted to do it by the book. This was both professional courtesy and because I planned to return for the 2022 World Cup to see how the country had progressed. In other words, I went into all of this with the best of intentions. It didn't quite work out like that.

Having spoken to colleagues who had previously left, and having in my possession the written instructions for navigating the inner working of this particular government organisation, I felt ready to tackle the HR bureaucracy. Three months later I was on a 'weekend trip' to Bahrain with no plans to ever return.

What follows is a timeline of those unfortunate events.

10 weeks out
Tell my director I am resigning. Hand in official notice. Transfer all money to offshore bank accounts.

9 weeks out
Hand in official paperwork to the CEO's office. The CEO needs to approve any resignation before the process can begin in earnest. Once this happens I'll be barred from leaving the country, stop receiving my income (it will be paid out in bulk at the end), and obliged to clear all debts before I can officially leave.

7 weeks out
Check with the CEO's office about approval. Nothing has been signed. Am told to come back a month before departure.

5 weeks out
Organise shipment of various bits and pieces back home with a freight company. I find a small Indian firm that can do it for a fraction of the price charged by international companies. Am pleasantly surprised when everyone arrives on time and in one piece a few weeks later.

4 weeks out
Check back with the CEO's office. Am told to come back next week. Speak to our in-house travel agency. Ask them to cash-in my flight home. I can book cheaper flights and pocket the difference.

3 weeks out
Check back with the CEO's office. Am told to come back next week.

2 weeks out
Sell all my 'big ticket' household items I can't take home, e.g. sofa, bed, etc. Check back with the CEO's office. Am told there is a huge stack of resignations waiting on his desk but he'll "get to them." Panic is starting to set in. I only have two weeks to get internal sign-off from five departments (housing, finance, etc.), and have been waiting two months for just the CEO's signature.

12 days out
Check back with the CEO's office. Am told all is under control and to come back tomorrow.

11 days out
Check back with the CEO's office. Am told everything is still under control and to check back tomorrow. Veins in my head are starting to bulge. Once the CEO approves my resignation I'm bared from leaving the country until the process is over. If everyone drags their feet like this I may be stuck in Qatar for weeks.

10 days out
Check back with the CEO's office. Am told everything is still under control and to check back tomorrow. Drive out the to the alcohol shop to get my deposit back on the liquor license.

9 days to go
Sell the remainder of my possessions over the weekend. Get desperate and call up some local thrift shops to come through and pillage the place. They offer me pennies on the dollar for whatever is left, but it's not like I have much choice. The apartment is now empty, aside from a duvet to sleep on, and some scattered books.

8 days to go
Check back with the CEO's office. Am told everything is still under control and to check back tomorrow. Lose. My. Mind. Realise that I'm dangerously close to being stranded in the country and at the whims of a HR department that simply doesn't care. Decide it's time to take matters into my own hands.

7 days to go
Spend the morning being driven around to various national agencies to cancel my power, water, telco accounts and claim back deposits. Head to the airport that same afternoon and buy a one-way ticket to neighbouring Bahrain. Tell the driver to help himself to anything left in the apartment. Make it through Qatari customs with my multi-exit travel permit*, breathe a sigh of relief as the plane takes off.

6 days to go
Catch a flight from Bahrain back to Australia. I've taken the week off from work to 'sort out my affairs'. Nobody aside from a few close friends knows I've left.

5 days to go
Receive an email from the CEO's office to let me know that my resignation has been accepted and that my ability to leave the country is now suspended until all the paperwork is in order, all debts repaid and the bureaucracy has lumbered through the motions. Thankfully, I'm already back in Australia.

3 days to go
I email my director to let her know that I've flown back to Australia for a family emergency and that I won't be returning. Let her know that I'm happy to finalise my exit process remotely.

1 day to go
My email account for work has suspended. Have to send all correspondence via my private email account.

Official final day
If I had hung around like a sucker I'd still be trying to get forms signed, organising official 'apartment inspections' for my work-provided accommodation and stuck in Qatar. Instead, I'm back in Australia for a week of R&R before flying to Hong Kong to start a new job.

3 months later
My settlement package from the government organisation is paid into my Qatari bank account. I immediately transfer the funds to a local account.

*Senior western expats are often granted 'multi-exit permits' from their employers. These allow unlimited overseas travel and mean you don't have to get official 'okay' every time you want to duck over to Dubai or take a work trip. They are highly prized, as they allow you to get out of the country quickly should you run over a bunch of people while drunk driving. Or whatever.

---The Epilogue---

Thanks and Goodnight

I left Qatar in early 2015 after three years working for a government organisation. By year's end most of the expats I knew had followed suite, either resigning or being made redundant.

While everyone had their reasons for leaving, I think we'd all agree that Qatar simply wasn't fun at that point. When the great wave of western expats arrived in 2011-2012, money was pouring from the sky, the Emir was actively pursuing a global soft power agenda and no project or idea was considered too outlandish for the small Gulf state. Arriving in Qatar during those halcyon days meant working on huge infrastructure projects that would shape the country, its skyline and society for decades to come.

By 2015, that was all over. The rapid decline in international oil prices — the country's primary source of revenue (down from USD $100 to $30 a barrel) — had left a huge gap in the country's finances. More importantly, the new Emir was a religious and fiscal conservative who favoured a more low-key, domestic policy. The budgetary shortfall was the perfect excuse to cancel a lot of expensive vanity projects from the previous administration.

And that's exactly what happened. Anything that wasn't related to the 2022 FIFA World Cup was either put on the backburner or quietly cancelled. Which is basically the same thing in Qatar, anyway. With no money, no projects, and nothing to work on, entire government departments found themselves collecting a pay cheque to show up and watch YouTube.

At the same time, it was made abundantly clear to the expats that our services were no longer needed or appreciated. Annual bonuses were cancelled, our travel allowances were cancelled and the various perks that helped justify life in a dusty construction site evaporated.

With no projects on the horizon, no perks, and our salaries actually going backwards most expats looked around, realised this wasn't what they had signed up for and planned their exit — official or otherwise.

That said, Qatar will rise again. With the FIFA World Cup six years away, and a huge amount of infrastructure still in the works, the country will ramp up its demand for foreign professionals in the near future.

Hopefully this book will help those new arrivals navigate the country a little better.

Section 6. Bars and Clubs Appendix

---The Bars and Clubs and Dives of Doha---

The Old Manor Bar at the Mercure

So I've been meaning to write this review for several months, but I keep getting distracted. It's just that there's SO MUCH to do in Doha, it's hard to actually sit down at a keyboard and start typing words because you might MISS OUT on the BEST NIGHT EVA. So many Best Nights! OMG!

Sorry, that's sarcasm. This review has been on the backburner due to being drunk a lot and not having the motor neuron skills to make the keys go click click click without sounding retarded. Also. Revenge! So much revenge…

Sorry (again), that's an in-joke that maybe two people in the world will get. It relates to an article that Vincent Gallo wrote about Vincent Gallo in a magazine published by the Beastie Boys. You can find it online. AND YOU REALLY SHOULD READ IT. Because then we can have a conversation about it if we ever meet in real life and not just stand there awkwardly looking around the room for someone better to talk to…

At this point it may be worth mentioning that numerous cans of Red Bull have been consumed prior to writing this. If you can get the caffeine dosage just right you achieved this unhinged stream of consciousness writing shtick that only lasts for 30 minutes before you crash and burn. So it's VERY IMPORTANT to write down all your thoughts as they occur or they'll be lost FOREVER. And maybe you'll die…

None of which has anything to do with the Old Manor, but we're about to get to that… So, okay, the Old Manor is sort of infamous. It's located at the top of the Mercure Hotel in Musheireb, which was maybe sort of 'okay' back in the 1995, but these days it's only really used to hide people's mistresses and illicit affairs when they're travelling to Qatar for 'work'. This is speculation, it's not like we've personally knocked on doors and asked people if they're staying there to have affairs. Artistic license, if you will…

Point is, the Mercure isn't a very nice hotel. Technically it says 'Five Stars' on the wall outside, but, yeah, nah. The Old Manor successfully maintains this low-rent atmosphere. While it's supposed to have a sort of 'classy' cigar lounge décor — bookshelves, armchairs and ornate wallpaper — the whole place looks like it's been dragged to hell and back. Basically, it's a dive. And like the best dive bars, anything goes.

Unlike most establishments in Doha, the door staff pay minimum attention to who goes in and what they're wearing (*read between the lines*), and because the drink prices are so wonderfully cheap, and the back alley ambiance so strong, you'll find yourself in all kinds of surreal situations. This may involve 'foreign nationals' threatening to glass each other, bar staff being forced to keep the bar open by a group of men who technically shouldn't be drinking, overly friendly greetings in the bathroom and a whole multi-colour spectrum of weirdness.

Really though, you have to see it for yourself, because anything written here will not do justice to the place. There's also the fact that a lot of what goes on shouldn't be written about in any kind of public forum. Because, reasons…

But hey, if you're in the market for a local dive bar to offset all those boring nights at the W Hotel then this will do the job nicely. Just remember – what happens at Old Manor stays at Old Manor…

Trader Vic's at The Hilton

The first time I went to Trader Vic's, no one had explained it to me, and it just seemed like a retro tinged restaurant with a bunch of random Spanish people dancing in the corner. I went inside, had a look around, was like 'nah', and went somewhere else.

It's only when I got dragged back a second time that I realised that there's an outdoor area by the water and that this is supposed be some sort of Tiki Bar / restaurant.

Now, as I understand it, a Tiki Bar is supposed to be a Polynesian-themed bar that serves rum-based cocktails in cool ceramic mugs and the staff set things on fire (preferably the drinks).

Trader Vic's décor is Polynesian by way of a garage sale from a Samoan family. Yeah, you can order zombies, they have some clapped out old chairs and the menu has been designed to mimic Polynesians themes, but it's like the proprietors ran out of energy at that point, went 'fuck this', and spent the rest of the afternoon watching *Surf's Up*, or thinking about LandCruisers. Or whatever people do.

Anyway, some random facts that I sort of remember, or imagined, because, really, what difference does it make… The décor makes a passing nod to the southeast before giving up and settling for South Florida retirement home instead.

The drinks are served in generic cocktail glasses (not on fire). The staff behind the bar are made to wear cheap Hawaiian shirts, which makes you feel embarrassed for them.

Oh, and if you want to actually get a drink, you'll have to line up at the bar for around 20 minutes, gradually losing the will to live.

So why do people come here on the regular? That would be the outdoor area alongside the water. There's a sort of boardwalk that juts out into the ocean and you can lean against it being cool, smoking cigarettes, drinking drinks and wondering why the DJ is playing old 80s songs. Also, talking to girls. Or guys. Or both. Or having crippling social anxiety and just looking at your phone all night! The possibilities are almost endless!

For real though, when the weather is just right, and the palm trees are swaying in the wind and you're on your third Tiki Puka Puka cocktail, this place can be pretty, pretty, okay. But the hangover will be hellish.

Crystal at W Hotel

If you've just arrived in Doha and are experiencing culture shock, Crystal should help. Housed within the W Hotel, it's a pretty good approximation of a sleazy nightclub anywhere in the west. Only with a lot of more volleyball players!

Qatar might be a conservative Muslim country, but the five-star hotels scattered throughout Doha are considered neutral zones. They're sorta like a foreign consulate — once you set foot inside, the normal rules don't apply. In other words, you can drink till you're drunk, wear short-ass dresses (dat ass!), go home with strangers and behave like a complete degenerate. It's a welcome novelty in Doha, but it does come with a number of caveats.

First up, you're going to pay for the privilege. The W wants to ensure they have the 'right' kind of expatriates all up in their shit, i.e. those with money. Before you can set foot in Crystal you have to buy yourself a six-month membership (200 QR, about USD $60). Get inside and the drinks are some of the most expensive you'll find in Doha. Expect to pay around 65 QR (USD $18) for the most basic drink. Oh, and if you want to sit down that's going to cost you extra.

The other thing to keep in mind is that Crystal doesn't want to have a bunch of dudes looking at each other til someone turns gay. Men are 'strongly encouraged' to show up with women to help keep the numbers inside even. If you're rolling with a crew of dudes, you ain't getting in.

Get past the security and you'll find yourself in a bad Flo-Rida video clip. There are lots of private booths, Top 40 club hits, and enough drinks with sparklers to [redacted because I don't want to get deported]…

There are also LOTS OF TALL DUDES. For some reason Qatar seems to think Volleyball is a real sport and imports a bunch of guys from other countries to compete locally. They all hang out at the W and hit on the flight attendants from Qatar Airways.

Point is, if you've been clubbing anywhere else in the world you've seen all this before. Only better. And while the dim lighting, professional staff and faux opulence try and disguise the reality, a photo of the crowd with the flash turned on will have you recoiling in horror.

The Ritz-Carlton

I'm not sure which Eastern European backwater The Ritz-Carlton imports its cocktail staff from, but they all seem to be on brain-rattling medication. Attempts to order items directly from the menu can turn into 10-minute ordeals and it's not uncommon for the staff to return several minutes later to confirm an incorrect order. Or they just never come back…

The shabby service is kind of a downer because the cocktail lounge is actually nice. It has a traditional Arabic theme (filtered through a western perspective), and the sort of sofas you can sink into like you just took a hit of heroin. Also, the menu is pretty decent.

If you're trying to stay sober (after several hazy years in Dubai?), there's a wide variety of mocktails, a very good Greek salad + chicken skewers combo, and a whole elaborate thing they do with tea. Seriously though, The Ritz-Carlton seems inordinately proud of their tea. They do this whole song and dance routine with it involving giant teapots (complete with cozies), and some fine china.

Unfortunately, it all falls apart when it comes to the proper cocktails. As in, they're just not very good. While they manage to get the basics right, i.e. a Martini glass for your Manhattan, the cocktails all taste pretty watered down… Obviously this misses the point. If you're ordering cocktails then you're out to get hammered. Or laid. Or both.

And that's the thing — The Ritz-Carlton lounge is at its best in the early afternoon. It's the sort of place you meet people before heading out properly. Or where you chill after spending time at the 11,000 QR (USD $3500) a year health club. Basically, it has a 'chill' vibe. And that doesn't really change whether you swing past at 5pm or 11pm.

Sky View at La Cigale

So I've tried to write (and rewrite) this review several times, but it just isn't working out. The problem, I think, is that I've been trying to base the entire review around a suicide joke.

Okay, I should probably explain that…

I figured I'd start the review by spending a couple of paragraphs talking up the place, explaining how it was a rooftop bar with great views and how it was a 'sophisticated' place to meet friends for a drink. I'd then dovetail into this whole thing about how you could also jump over the railings and kill yourself if you didn't have friends… Only, you know, I wrote it 'funny'.

Having gotten the suicide joke out of the way, I'd then end with something like,
"Oh yeah, they have a cover charge on weekends. It's around 200 QR (USD $70) just to set foot in the place after 10pm. I guess that's to encourage 'the right sort of people'. You can avoid that indignity by getting there earlier in the evening. And with both 7 Nightclub and Piano Bar also located at La Cigale, it's actually the perfect spot to get drunk before you have to face the horrors of Doha's club scene."

Obviously this is a terrible premise for a review. So if anyone can write a decent bar review of Sky View please get in contact. Until then…

Champions at The Marriot

If you're a 'bro' and looking for a sports bar then this is probably your best bet in Doha. Which isn't really saying much…

As the name implies, Champions is one of these modern sports bars where everything is shiny, neon lit and utterly soulless. The last refugee of the damned if you want to get all melodramatic about it.

Maybe it's just me, but I don't get why all sports bars have to look like shit nightclubs these days. When I picture a sports bar I think of some Boston dive with a beat-up television in the corner screening baseball games, old Budweiser signs from the 80s cluttering the walls and off-duty Irish cops knocking back whiskey shots with beer chasers.

But I digress; Champions is bright, modern and has giant photos of Formula 1 cars on the walls. They also have lots of plasmas scattered throughout the venue. Curiously, all they seem to show is football (soccer). At any given moment there might be 3-4 different games on various screens. This can be quite disconcerting if you're hammered.

One good thing about Champions is that the booze is actually pretty reasonably priced. Beers will run you about 30-35QR (USD $10) and scotch is in the same ballpark. If you're going out to a proper bar later in the evening you can get a nice buzz going here for under 100QR (USD $30).

They also have a reasonably priced bar menu. I can't vouch for the quality of the food because the 'waiter' who took our order failed to actually pass it on to anyone. When we enquired about our food after 40 minutes we were meet with blank stares and told it would be another hour before anything arrived because they were 'hella busy'. Based on this fact (and because they wouldn't give us a free round by way of apology), I'm going to go ahead and say the food is awful.

Oh, and the crowd is pretty grim too. As you'd imagine the ratio is heavily skewed towards dudes. Especially old dudes. If you're looking to meet your 'life partner' than this isn't the place. Unless of course you're looking for an overweight white guy in his 50s who hangs out in sports bars.

So yeah, Champions sucks. But it's still the best sports bar in Doha.

The Sharq

If you really want to embrace a decadent expat lifestyle, The Sharq pool bar is an excellent place to start. It's stupid, overpriced and ridiculous. Kinda like Doha.

At 350 QR (USD $120) per day to gain admission, it's one of the most expensive hotel beaches in the country. And while that kind of money might be justified if the Sharq was on some next-level-shit, it's actually sub-par on several counts. Let's list them:

1. It's located right next to the airport and directly underneath the flight path. A Boeing 747 will roar overhead every ten minutes or so. You half expect each of these planes to crash into your deck chair and kill you.

2. The beach is kinda crappy. You're basically going to be looking out at a sprawling commercial port and oil tankers on the horizon. Neither of these suggests 'clean waters'. Which is probably why no one ever goes swimming at the beach. Instead people hang out in the pool.

3. The Sharq Village & Spa is comprised of numerous small villas grouped together. There's nothing technically wrong with that, but it also feels like you're hanging out in a residential apartment complex rather than a five-star hotel.

4. The pool area is filled with assholes. Due to all the above issues, no self-respecting person in Doha would hang out here. That just leaves people who think it's a good idea to hang out in overpriced hotel pools with crap views. Do you want to be friends with these people? Um, no.

Okay, to be fair, it's not all bad. The pool does have a swim-up bar so you can get weird on cocktails while half submerged in water. There's a certain bent appeal to that. Also, there's the … no, wait, that's it.

So yeah, The Sharq pool bar is filled with assholes that believe going to the worst beach / most expensive pool in the country is an acceptable lifestyle choice. If you feel like blowing huge wads of cash to join them, go for it. For everyone else, there's The Sheraton, Four Seasons and Intercon. All of which provide better views and beaches for less money.

Jazz Bar at the Rotana

The Jazz Bar is worth visiting just for the sliders. You won't find a better mini burger anywhere in Doha. Seriously, I don't know what their secret is, but they make every other mini burger in town taste like ass. Also, they're cheap — two burgers for 55 QR (about USD $15).

Okay, sorry about that. Let's try and be sensible about this… The Jazz Bar is located within the Rotana Hotel (near the old airport) and, as the name suggests, it's a jazz bar. It's also a welcome change of pace from Doha's sleazy nightclubs and cocktail bars. This is a place where you can sit on couple's lounges, drink cocktails, eat mini burgers (sorry) and watch a live band run through some questionable 'classics'.

For what it's worth, the house band are actually pretty good. Well, the guys on the instruments. The vocalists tend to change every month, so that aspect is a bit hit and miss. On bad nights it can feel like dodgy karaoke, i.e. *Mustang Sally*, but they'll also throw in stuff like Sade's *Smooth Operator*. So, you know…

Anyway, the interior is minimal and sleek (rare for Qatar), with a heavy emphasis on low-slung swivel chairs grouped in pairs. Throw in some dim lighting, a large cocktail list (including 60 QR (USD $16) shots of Patron), and you can see why it's a popular venue for third dates.

Basically, if you're in living in Doha and don't hate jazz music you should visit. You should bring a date. And you should try the sliders.

Four Seasons Cigar Lounge

The Cigar Lounge at the Four Seasons Doha makes the best cocktails in town. Let's just get that out of the way up front. If you're serious about your Manhattans, or your Hemmingway Daquiris or whatever the hell it is you drink, the bar staff here actually know what they're doing. Compared to the crap that other 5 Star hotels try to pass of as cocktails Four Seasons is a life raft for the seasoned drinker.

It's also very nice inside. If you're looking for that classic, understated elegance steez then this is the spot. Combining polished wooden surfaces, green felt and armchairs that wouldn't look out of place in *Alice in Wonderland*, it's the sort of hotel lounge where you can discuss high-powered business merges and also get your date drunk in a relaxed environment.

Oh, and since it's technically a cigar lounge they have, you know, cigars. All of which adds to that 'I'm successful and I can afford to get drunk on cocktails mid-week' vibe.

I'd write something negative about the bar at this point to balance things out a little bit, but I can't really think of anything. Granted, you're going to find an older crowd here — if you want to pick up hookers then you're better of sticking with The W — but that's hardly a deal breaker.

Also! If you do get drunk / hungry, you can wonder down to the beach lounge and order the best chimichangas in town (deep fried burritos if you don't know). Essentially, I'm super gay for Four Seasons and want to marry it.

Waterhole at the Sheraton

[Note – the Sheraton was renovated in 2015, presumably they set the old Waterhole bar on fire and never spoke of it again.]

Do not come here. Ever. Never-ever-ever-ever come here. Do not set foot in this place. Do not joke about coming here. I cannot emphasise enough how much you should avoid Waterhole. It is not only the worst dive in all of Doha, it's quite possibly the worst bar in the entire world. The sort of place where dreams come to knock-back one last shot of alcohol before quietly dying in the corner.

For serious though. Do not come here. The décor looks like it hasn't been updated since the Sheraton was originally built in 1979 (FYI, it's Doha's oldest hotel). The couches look like they were dragged in from the side of the road, the actual bar has those neon signs that were cheap and tacky back in the 80s, and the general ambiance is not unlike a third-world whore house in the middle of a warzone.

Speaking of whore houses; if you're in the market for haggard Filipino hookers the wrong side of 40 then you're in luck. Where did they all come from? And why is one of them wearing a Phil Collins *Groovy Kind of Love* t-shirt. Also, they are mean. Try and take a photo of the hookers and they will try to fight you.

The guys, meanwhile, are an entirely bewildering mix of flamboyantly gay Indians, black dudes wearing Klue Jeans and fake Timbalands like it was 1992, and sleazy British guys in their 50s with the aforementioned hookers on their laps. A special shout-out to the dude at the front entrance pleading with security to let him in — even thought he's wearing a tennis outfit.

Oh, and the security are great. While most places would frown upon middle-aged Arab men lying passed out on couches, around here no one bats an eyelid. And to really add insult to injury, they actually charge five-star hotel prices for their drinks. And the drinks are filled with poison! Probably.

Waterhole is truly, unequivocally, God Awful, and the Sheraton hotel chain should be ashamed of itself for allowing this place to exit. To reiterate — unless you're into truly heavy irony, avoid this place at all costs.

Belgian Beer Café at the InterContinental

Every city in the world has a Belgian Beer Bar. And they all look pretty much identical. I suspect there's a massive warehouse somewhere in China that specialises in faux Belgian fittings. It's probably right next door to the one that sells products for 'authentic' Irish pubs.

Point is, if you've been in a 'Belgian Beer Bar' you'll know what to expect. It's a casual mix of wooden bar stools, shiny brass, overly elaborate beer pouring techniques, booth seats and a bunch of other incidental details too dull to mention.

What's weird about the Doha branch is the insane ratio of white dudes having dinner with attractive Asian women. And I don't mean the random hookers you'll find scattered around some of the city's more dubious establishments. The women here are, for the most part, professional, well dressed, yada, yada.

All of which can be very distracting if you're single. Where are these men finding all these attractive Asian women? Is there a website? A secret club? Why aren't I having dinner with an attractive Asian lady?

Aside from that particular mystery, the crowd tends to consist of British ex-pat caricatures. Between the shaved heads, pale skin and popped collars on rugby jerseys they couldn't look any more British if they tried. Oh, and the atmosphere is rowdy, pub-like — a little taste of British pub culture in the middle of the desert.

On that note, if you're a fan of beer this place has one of Doha's widest selections. Aside from the obligatory Hoegarden they have, well, lots and lots of imported beers. I don't know / care enough about beer to list them all, but there's a bunch of imported top shelf stuff you won't find elsewhere. And they all have their special glasses — which is nice. You can soak up the booze with a reasonably priced selection of pub meals.

Basically, if you're looking for a fake / authentic pub experience in Doha then you should go here. And if you can figure out the deal with the hot Asian women on dates please let me know. Thx.

Paloma at the InterContinental

I have a friend who insists on dragging me down here. It'll get to around 11pm at night, we'll be a few drinks in and she'll insist on visiting Paloma. I'll bitch and moan and offer several alternatives, but inevitably we'll end up here — standing by the bar ordering tequila shots to make it all seem less horrible.

And that's the thing about Paloma, you really need to be drunk to deal with its 'ambiance'. This may have something to do with the fact it's a Mexican restaurant by day, a live music venue in the early evening and, eventually, a nightclub.

The fact it has no cover charge and one of the most laidback door policies in Doha makes for a pretty terrifying crowd. It's a mix of working-class African guys, short Filipino women, a handful of slightly bewildered white guys and a room full of sexually ambiguous Arab men dancing to terrible house music in the back room.

The good thing about this combination is that no one can possibly judge you here. So Paloma is the bar where people get drunk, dance to (bad) hip hop in the front room, truly awful house in the back, try to pick up, and knock back tequila shots at the bar to drown out the horror.

Question is: Are you drunk enough to dance to Lil Jon in a converted Mexican restaurant?

The Rugby Club

The Rugby Club has one of the most exclusive door policies in Doha. Which is ironic, because it's also one of the biggest shitholes… While most Doha venues let you sign up on the door, The Rugby Club seems to have delusions of grandeur. You have to register online several weeks ahead, submit a photo of yourself passed out drunk in a ditch, and speak like you were dragged up in a Glasgow methadone clinic before they'll even let you in.

Alternatively, you can have a member sign you in. Since I obviously don't have the patience to go through the official procedure, I simply showed up and found some random 'bros' with popped collars and memberships that were willing to let me in. That plan quickly unravelled when we reached the front door and their were #dramaz about how many people could be signed in and blah, blah, blah.

'Rules' are obviously for suckers, so I simply waited until everybody was distracted by the yelling and slipped in through a side door. This seemed like an excellent alternative until I was approached by security, escorted out and banned for life. It then took another half hour of, "Okay, I'm very sorry, if I'm nice and respectful can you please make an exception and let me in tonight?" before they relented and turned me loose inside their shitty venue.

The thing you have to keep in mind is that the Rugby Club is an anomaly in Doha.
In a city where your only public drinking options are five-star hotels, The Rugby Club is the sort of back alley dive that would make Irvine Welsh blush. A place where British nationals drink lager till they pass out and the girls end the evening with their heels in a bin and their mascara smeared with tears. Oh, and they charge 800 QR (USD $220) per year for the privilege.

So what does your membership get you? Glad you asked. The Rugby Club is basically a football pitch, a covered outdoor shed and a small community hall with the saddest dance floor this side of a high school disco for pregnant teens. Ignoring well-established conventions, the proprietors prefer to keep the lights on inside the venue, illuminating the dance floor like a late night car crash, and making no attempts to disguise the chairs and tables they've stacked up in the corner, or the raffle wheel or the not very attractive people shuffling around awkwardly to the mix-CD blaring through the PA.

Step outside and it's just a bunch of random white people on raised bar stools drinking beer. Which is about as interesting as it sounds, so let's just skip ahead and mention the VERY reasonable drink prices. If the Rugby Club has one saving grace it's that you can get BLACK OUT DRUNK for a fraction of what it would cost you elsewhere. Four shots of (terrible) tequila will set you back around 100 QR (USD $30), and probably have you waking up in bed with a strange woman who's name you do not recall, used condoms flung around the room and your semen stains on the curtains. If you're a woman you'll have inadvertently made a baby with a random Irish dude who's missing teeth.

Of course you're not supposed to take the Rugby Club seriously. Because God help you if you think hanging out here is a reasonable lifestyle choice. This is heavy irony taken to its drunken extreme. A tin shed in the middle of the desert where you can watch British expats revert to their most primal state; the best / worst shit-show in town.

Level 23 at The Ritz-Carlton

[Note — the original review was mostly drunken gibberish about how the foyer at this upscale hotel bar sort of looks like The Black Lodge in *Twin Peaks*. The review then immediately contradicted itself by clarifying that this wasn't true, and that the writer just felt like talking about *Twin Peaks*. It was basically a complete mess, so this picks up after all the *Twin Peaks* nonsense has been dealt with...]

For whatever reason, the staff seem to believe that a scotch on ice is actually a full glass of scotch, with a couple cubes of ice for good measure. When you combine this with their 2-4-1 deals on Thursday afternoon, the potential to imagine you're in TV show from early 90s is VERY HIGH.

But to be honest, there's nothing that exciting about Level 23. Walk into the venue proper and there are chairs and stuff, a bar off in the corner and great views of The Pearl. It's all very nice, good for dates and they have an impressive selection of whisky, but those kinda mundane details are hardly going to win me a Pulitzer.

Printed in Poland
by Amazon Fulfillment
Poland Sp. z o.o., Wrocław